Caroline Zoob

with photography by Caroline Arber

Foreword by Cecil Woolf

Virginia Woolf's Garden

The story of the garden at Monk's House

jacqui small

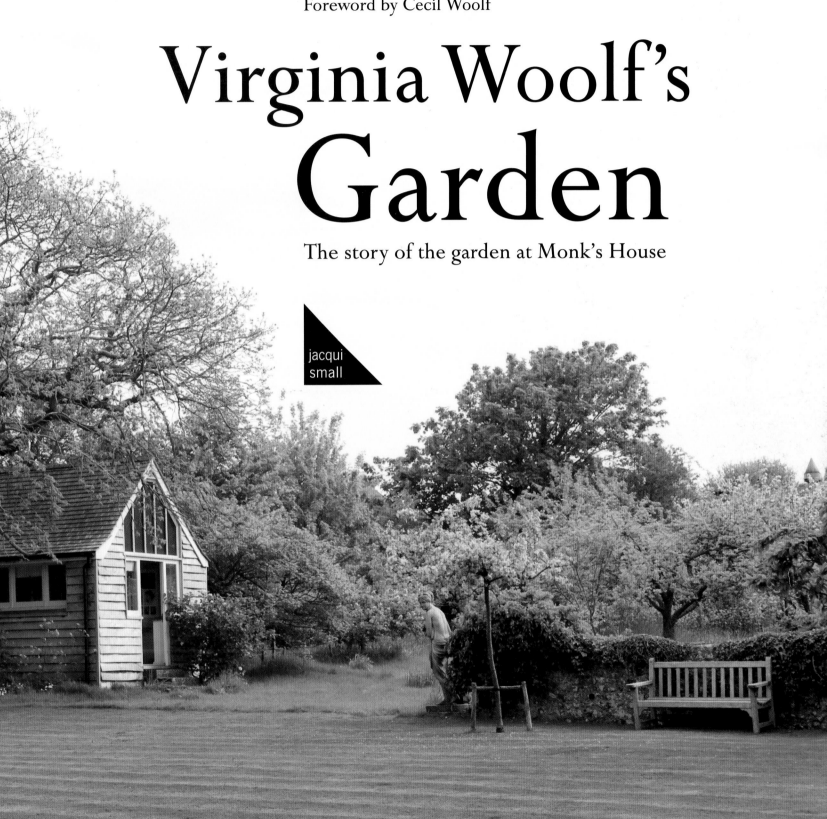

First published in 2013 by
Jacqui Small LLP
An imprint of Aurum Press
74–77 White Lion Street
London N1 9PF
www.jaquismallpub.com

First published in the USA in 2013

Publisher: Jacqui Small
Associate Publisher: Joanna Copestick
Managing Editor: Lydia Halliday
Designer: Maggie Town
Editor: Sian Parkhouse
Illustrator: Lorna Brown
Embroidered illustrations: Caroline Zoob
Production: Peter Colley

ISBN: 978 1 909342 13 2

A catalogue record for this book is
available from the British Library.

2015 2014 2013
10 9 8 7 6 5 4 3 2 1

Printed in China

Virginia Woolf's
Garden

This book is dedicated to everyone who has toiled, even briefly, in the garden at Monk's House, but especially to my husband Jonathan
CAROLINE ZOOB

To my husband Bob – a wonderful gardener and grower
CAROLINE ARBER

Contents

Foreword

I HAVE BEEN TRAVELLING BACK IN MEMORY through some seven crowded decades, to when, as a schoolboy before the Second World War, I had the pleasure of staying at Monk's House with my uncle and aunt, Leonard and Virginia Woolf. Leonard was one of my father's older brothers.

It must have been in about 1936 that I first spent a weekend at that charming house and garden. I retain a picture in my mind's eye of arriving at Monk's House and pushing open the creaking wooden gate, which was the signal for what seemed like a pack of excited but friendly dogs to bound down the brick path that ran along the end of the house. Leonard would perhaps emerge from a greenhouse to greet me with his warm smile and firm handshake. He is in his sixties, of medium height, lean, tanned, with a shock of silver hair. His eyes are grey and his face is deeply lined. His head, which juts forward, is chiselled, long and spare. He has the profile of an Old Testament prophet smoking a pipe. He is wearing ancient corduroy trousers and a shabby poacher jacket of coarse tweed. His shoes are made of good leather. On his shoulder is perched a tiny monkey, a marmoset called Mitzi. Virginia, interrupted by the barking of the dogs, strolls across the lawn from her little writing cabin.

It would take an horticultural epic – for which my abilities as a poet and my knowledge as a gardener are unequal – to do full justice to the little Eden I remember. Leonard and Virginia had no children: their books and their garden were their children. My recollections of the garden are inevitably somewhat impressionistic. From the overgrown land behind the house that the Woolfs had bought twenty years earlier, they had created a spectacular mosaic of brightly coloured flowers – cinerarias of many colours, vast white and flaming orange lilies, dahlias, carnations and a riot of red hot pokers – merging into vegetables, gooseberry bushes, pear trees, apple trees, figs. Here and there on the lawn were scattered goldfish ponds. Besides the flower garden and orchard, there were the beehives and the greenhouses, where Leonard had an extensive collection of cacti and succulents.

Unlike the grand and formal gardens at Sissinghurst, created by Virginia's close friend Vita Sackville-West, the Woolfs' garden was organic, delightfully informal and less self-conscious. The garden at Monk's House was a collaborative enterprise.

While Leonard was the driving force, and rightly given the main credit for it, it is evident both from Virginia's books and diaries that gardens and open spaces played a significant part in her life. She loved the garden and, as I clearly recall, played her part in the multitude of tasks that go to making an enchanted domain.

Leonard, by the time I stayed at Monk's, had become an expert horticulturalist; his interest in the subject had, I think, started during the seven years he spent as a colonial administrator in Ceylon, and continued until his death. Even into his eighties he was still an enthusiastic and energetic gardener.

Gardening was not just a pleasure in itself, but also a means of unwinding after a week spent in London, pursuing their careers: Virginia as a writer, publisher and pivotal figure in the Bloomsbury group, and Leonard as a publisher, writer and editor. Here, too, overlooking the Sussex Downs, they could relax with their friends and talk – and talk prodigiously – and play bowls.

Turning over the pages of photographs that follow not only brings back memories of long-ago visits before and after the war, after Virginia's death, but reminds me of all the hard work that, following a long period of neglect, has gone into restoring the garden to something like it was when Leonard and Virginia tended it so lovingly.

Cecil Woolf
February 2013

'... what has the deepest and most permanent effect upon oneself and one's way of living is the house in which one lives. The house determines the day-to-day, hour-to-hour, minute-to-minute quality, colour, atmosphere, pace of one's life; it is the framework of what one does, of what one can do, and of one's relations with people.' Leonard Woolf

Introduction

AT THE NORTHERNMOST END of the Sussex village of Rodmell, 'dropped beneath the Downs', lies a long, narrow, weather-boarded house, close to the street above a flint wall. Mentioned in the Manor Court rolls for the first time at the beginning of the eighteenth century, it was home to a procession of carpenters and millers until, on 1 July 1919, it was sold at auction to a Mr Leonard Sidney Woolf.

Behind the house is a garden, the story of which is the subject of this book. It is not a large garden. Secluded behind flint walls and yew hedges with the grey spire of St Peter's Church rising over its orchard, it is significant because Monk's House was the country home of Leonard and his wife, Virginia, two of the most important literary figures of the twentieth century. Monk's House was not Virginia's only garden. The garden at Talland House in St Ives, Cornwall, where she spent childhood holidays, was the fount of some of her most significant memories. But Monk's House was the garden of her writing life. For twenty-two years she worked on most of her novels in her writing lodge tucked into a corner of the orchard. In periods of the illness and depression that plagued her throughout her life, the deep peace of the garden and the quiet routine of country life helped to soothe her mind. When she was well and writing, the garden was a source of inspiration. Even the morning walk across the garden to reach her writing lodge was an important part of her creative routine.

After Virginia took her own life by drowning, in 1941, Leonard Woolf remained at Monk's House until his own death in 1969. Over the course of the half century he spent there he created the garden remembered so vividly by Cecil Woolf in the preceding foreword.

I lived at Monk's House with my husband, Jonathan, for ten years as tenants of the National Trust, who have owned and managed the house since 1980. We planted and tended the garden as other tenants had done before us, and opened the house to the public two afternoons a week for seven months of the year. Rather like the Woolfs in 1919, we had very little gardening experience but plenty of enthusiasm. So much has been written about every aspect of their lives that it seems impossible that anything new can be added. Some of the material in this

OPPOSITE This photograph captures what it feels like to be in the garden at Monk's House, the brick paths beckoning through tunnels of lush foliage to the next garden room. The old pear tree long ago resigned itself to standing and serving as host to a *Clematis montana*. Below some irises very similar to *Iris sibirica* 'Royal Blue' and *Gladioli communis* subsp. *byzantinus* mix with frothy *Alchemilla mollis*.

book can be found in corners of other, more scholarly, books, but this is the
first book to put the garden centre stage, both through the text and the
photographs by Caroline Arber, a friend and frequent visitor to the house over
the years of our occupancy.

Over seven chapters, the book tells the story of how the garden has evolved
since 1919, when the Woolfs found the house, to the present day. A certain
amount of biographical information about the Woolfs is included, and at the end
of each section the different garden rooms are described in detail.

Leonard and Virginia were fascinated by the idea of a 'quiet continuity of
people living'[1], believing that the people who had lived in the house before
them had been absorbed into its history, each playing a small part in creating
the 'tranquil atmosphere' of the house and garden. The sense of this is greater
when a house and garden do not change very much over the years. Had Monk's
House been sold on the open market in 1969, it would by now have been gutted,
sandblasted and gentrified beyond recognition. The convoluted surface piping
and wiring would have been buried and the marks of the house's rich human
history smoothed out under new plaster. Instead, living there, we moved through
the same spaces as the Woolfs, trod on the same worn steps, banged our heads
on the same beams and, most of all, opened the curtains each day to see the
garden spread out below, still shaped according to Leonard's inspiration around
the crumbling remains of piggeries and outbuildings, the eye still led by the brick
paths he set down nearly a century ago.

Caroline Zoob
Author and former tenant at Monk's House

THIS PAGE The garden, taken at sunrise, from the balcony of 'Hedgehog Hall', the narrow study carved out of the attics in 1938 for Leonard. When Leonard and Virginia bought Monk's House, none of the borders or brick paths existed and the area between the foreground and the orchard was lawn. In place of the tree with the clematis there was a small laundry and behind, an earth closet shrouded in cherry laurels. The church of St Peter's dates from the 12th century.

Church Twitten leading to St Peter's Church

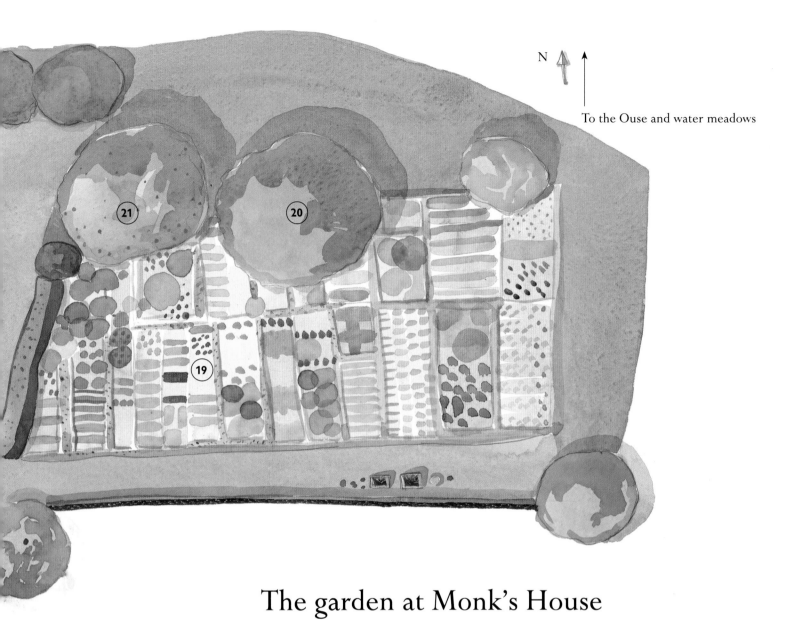

To the Ouse and water meadows

The garden at Monk's House

Part 1 Finding Monk's House

In 1919 Leonard and Virginia Woolf had been married for seven years. They were dividing their time between Hogarth House in Richmond, where they had started the Hogarth Press in 1917, and Asheham, a mysteriously beautiful Regency villa with graceful windows and views across the Ouse Valley to the village of Rodmell. Their first novels had been well received and they were 'blossoming out' as printers, with the Hogarth Press having recently published a slim volume of poems by a young American poet called Thomas Stearns Eliot. Virginia had just finished her second novel, *Night and Day*, and had started to recover from the traumatic mental breakdowns and suicide attempt which had shadowed the early years of the Woolfs' marriage.

ABOVE Leonard Woolf and Virginia Stephen during their engagement in 1912.
OPPOSITE The exterior of Monk's House today. Leonard commissioned the gate in 1929, to be 'absolutely plain oak without any ornamentation at all'[1]. *Rosa* 'Moonlight' tumbles over the flint wall.

ABOVE The conveyance of the house in 1919 was the first time the name Monk's House was used. No hard evidence for the provenance of the name has been unearthed. Previous inhabitants once lived at Monks Gate. To use or not to use an apostrophe: in letters and diaries the Woolfs varied, and it was always used on headed stationery, although not on the gate.

ABOVE RIGHT Monk's House in 1919. Leonard removed the stone pillars and leaning wall in 1929, with the latter replaced by a wooden fence.

OPPOSITE The Orchard in September. This plot has been the site of an established orchard for nearly two hundred years.

Virginia had always appreciated regular retreats to the country. While spending Christmas 1910 at The Pelham Arms in Lewes, she declared herself 'violently in favour of a country life. I like walking and coming back for tea . . . and then writing over the fire . . .'[2] When the owner of Asheham was unable to extend the lease after the end of the First World War it was a blow. Virginia loved the romance of Asheham and had started to 'dig in', entertaining friends, making blackberry jam and the first tentative attempts at gardening. Asheham was also a place where she and Leonard had grown close, finding it on one of the long walks they took during the first days of their friendship, and spending the first week of their honeymoon there in August 1912. A large part of Virginia's convalescence from her 1915 breakdown had been spent at Asheham, cared for by Leonard, nurses and close friends. It was clear to Leonard that periods of quiet country life, following a peaceful routine, were to be an essential part of avoiding further breakdowns. It was for this reason he had moved their London base to Richmond in 1915, believing that the perennial stimulation of life in Bloomsbury militated against Virginia's recovery. Now they had to look for a new country home.

In June 1919, during one of Leonard's rare absences, Virginia viewed and was rather taken with the Round House, part of a former mill, squeezed into a narrow twitten, or alleyway, in Lewes. On an impulse she made an offer, which was accepted. A few weeks later she and Leonard returned to Lewes to inspect their purchase. Walking up Station Street they noticed a poster announcing the sale by auction of 'Monk's House, Rodmell, an old-fashioned house standing in three quarters of an acre of land to be sold with possession'. 'That would have suited us exactly,' said Leonard, which must have filled Virginia with dismay since the Round House could not have been more different. They would have known Monk's House from their walks over Itford Hill from Asheham to the village shop in Rodmell to buy tobacco and provisions. Peeping over the long flint wall running from the lych gate of St Peter's Church they would have seen the Orchard, tended then by old Jacob Verrall, in mourning for his late wife and slowly starving himself to death. Although Leonard was polite about the Round House, Virginia could see

'... I could fancy a very pleasant walk
in the orchard under the apple trees,
with the grey extinguisher of the
church steeple pointing my boundary.'
Virginia Woolf

ABOVE The fireplace in the green drawing room with its arched niches 'for holy water'. In the cupboard below the niche on the left are the remains of a bread oven, used to bake bread by the Glazebrook family in the mid-nineteenth century.

The bill of sale shows that Leonard bought:

a 24 round ladder

12 kale pots

a hen coop and a quantity of
    flower pots

4 large apple trays

a Capital wheelbarrow

a stone garden roller

digging fork, prong, two hoes,
rake, spade and a pair of shears

he was not enthusiastic. It was an unseasonably cold, grey week and the Round House, which had seemed so charmingly quirky to Virginia only weeks before, now felt small, cramped and lacking in garden.

The following day Virginia bicycled to Rodmell against a biting wind, resolving this time to be more objective. She listed the faults to herself. The rooms at Monk's House were small, and while she could not resist romanticising the arched niches on either side of the fireplace as being 'for holy water' she made herself discount their charm. She noted the distinct lack of comforts and yet all attempts to be objective were forced to 'yield place to a profound pleasure at the size & shape & fertility & wildness of the garden. There seemed an infinity of fruit bearing trees; the plums crow[d]ed so as to weight the tip of the branch down; unexpected flowers sprouted among cabbages. There were well kept rows of peas, artichokes, potatoes; raspberry bushes had pale little pyramids of fruit; & I could fancy a very pleasant walk in the orchard under the apple trees, with the grey extinguisher of the church steeple pointing my boundary.'[3]

Virginia bicycled home and, forcing herself to suppress her excitement, told Leonard about her visit. The next day they went together to view the house and this time the enthusiasm was mutual. In his third volume of autobiography, *Beginning Again*, Leonard remembered that 'The orchard was lovely and the garden was the kind I like, much subdivided into a kind of patchwork quilt of trees, shrubs, flowers, vegetables, fruit, roses and crocus tending to merge into cabbages and currant bushes.'[4]

The auction was held at The White Hart on Tuesday 1 July 1919. Virginia recalled looking at the other bidders 'for signs of opulence, & was cheered to discover none'. Monk's House became the property of Mr Leonard Sidney Woolf as the hammer came down on the final bid of £700, Virginia 'purple in the cheeks, & L[eonard] trembling like a reed'[5].

One of the terms of the contract of sale for Monk's House was that an auction of the contents could be held in the garden. This was set for 14 August 1919 and was attended by the Woolfs. Apart from some curtain rods, a brass and wire fender (which is still in the house today) and a few household sundries, Leonard's focus was clearly on the garden (see the list from the bill of sale left). Letters and diary entries by Virginia immediately after buying Monk's House fizz with enthusiasm. They announced the purchase to friends with as much excitement as one might place a birth announcement in *The Times*: 'our address will be Monk's House, with niches for the holy water, and a great fireplace; but the point of it is the garden. I shan't tell you though, for you must come and sit there on the lawn with me, or stroll in the apple orchard, or pick – there are cherries, plums, pears, figs, together with all the vegetables. This is going to be the pride of our hearts; I warn you.'[6]

'. . . the plums crowded so as to weight the tip of the branch down' Virginia Woolf

'. . . there are cherries, plums, pears, figs, together with all the vegetables. This is going to be the pride of our hearts; I warn you.' Virginia Woolf

Part 2 Settling in

The key to Monk's House was left for the Woolfs by Jacob Verrall's sister on 18 August 1919 with a note hoping that 'you and Mrs Woolf will learn to love the little house as much as our dear brother did he simply adored it and enjoy the surroundings and fruit'. They moved in on 1 September, after harvest, the local farmer making two trips in his farm cart, clattering over the wooden bridge at Southease with the Woolfs' furniture and bundles of books and papers painstakingly tied up by Leonard. Now began the business of settling in.

ABOVE The top end of the kitchen today. The range would have been in the niche on the left. The recess used to be a window before the extension was built.
OPPOSITE A 'house of many doors'. The oak step beyond the bricks is worn with use.

RIGHT Taken in 1970, this is the only photograph showing the kitchen as it was before the National Trust fitted a new kitchen for tenants. In all other respects, including the bowed ceiling and labyrinthine piping, it remains the same. Nowadays, this part of the kitchen is used by the occupier of the house and is hidden behind a screen.
OPPOSITE The window was installed in 1937 to replace the one which used to be in the recess to the left of this picture. Virginia painted this room a vivid green. Traces of it can be found in the Heal's oak dresser.
BELOW Portrait of Louie Mayer (née Everest) by Trekkie Ritchie. Louie worked as the Woolfs' cook for over thirty years until Leonard's death.

The house took priority. There was no electricity, running water, bathroom or lavatory, and only an earth closet buried in a group of cherry laurels in the garden, so grim that the agent had refused to show it to them. Virginia embraced frosty morning excursions to the 'romantic chamber . . . down a winding glade'. Leonard, ever more pragmatic, rigged up a cane chair over a bucket in the loft.

In 1919, the Woolfs were certainly not poor but they were not yet comfortably off. Virginia's illness had forced them to abandon the economical lifestyle they had planned for the early years of their marriage. To pay doctors' fees Virginia had sold some of her jewellery. At the lowest point of her breakdown two nurses were required at all times in case of the need to restrain her physically, and Leonard was forced to ask for an advance on payments from her trust fund. Plans to earn their living by writing had also been affected by her illness, with publication of Virginia's first novel, *The Voyage Out*, postponed by over a year. Thus in the early years at Monk's House they did not have the funds to do more than put it into barely acceptable order. The kitchen was an immediate source of despair. On their first night water streamed under the steps from the garden and down the steeply sloping floor to run away through the scullery down a crack at the far end over the street. There were 'enormous rats' and the kitchen floor 'sweated' with damp. 'Move – whole horror of the process. One get's one furniture in but as for living in it – Then the kitchen was flooded the first night; the servants had hysterics; they packed their boxes . . . to have left Asheham was bad enough. I can't altogether get over that, although Leonard infinitely prefers this, chiefly on account of the garden, which pours pears and plums and apples and vegetables upon us.'[1]

The scullery and kitchen were knocked into one room and a Kitchener range stove (forebear of the Aga) installed. Virginia tentatively pronounced the

resulting kitchen a success, but conceded that she was not the cook. Nellie Boxall, who was, had a hard time of it. The stove had to be lit and maintained with heavy coal for the simplest of cooking tasks. Water had to be pumped by hand and heated on the stove. For the next five years Virginia and Leonard took their Rodmell baths in a tin tub behind a curtain in the kitchen. Virginia recalls making bread and watching the window 'lest Mrs Dedman finds L in his bath'[2]. As Nellie put it in an interview for the BBC in 1956, 'It was bread one end and bath the other!' Bizarrely, the Woolfs chose to return to freezing Rodmell to recover from the 'flu in January 1920, Virginia touchingly describing it as 'nicer than all London rolled in one here'.[3] Conditions at Monk's House until 1926 were primitive beyond the imaginings of people used to modern standards of convenience and comfort. Yet the Woolfs exhorted friends to experience the endurance test of a stay there; 'beds abound' she wrote to Lytton Strachey shortly after moving in, and to T.S. Eliot in September 1920: 'Please bring no clothes: we live in a state of the greatest simplicity.'[4] T.S. Eliot visited Monk's House several times, by far the most smartly dressed of their visitors. Mr Eliot became Tom and the friendship grew and endured.

Leonard was quick to claim the garden. The Woolfs had started to garden a little at Asheham, their inexperience revealed in a plea for advice from Virginia about 'starting a kitchen garden – with the hope of one day eating our own growing. Does this take long, and need great care? Any hints would be welcome, as there is no gardener. As to flowers, we have sown seeds in soap boxes filled with earth. Is this right?'[5] They achieved some success for later Leonard reported that 'the garden has produced 1 cwt. Potatoes, some broad beans, French beans, Japanese anemones, nasturtia, phlox and dahlias and a forest of weeds. I spend nearly every afternoon in it.'[6] Now, at Monk's House, the first task was to harvest and sell all the growing crops of pears, apples, potatoes, cabbages, parsnips, carrots and onions, valued at £22 12s on the day of the house clearance auction. Virginia had predicted that Leonard would become a 'fanatical lover' of the garden and soon wrote that 'Leonard has become what I daresay is called garden proud. We can't resist going out to look at pears, and then the potatoes have to be weighed . . . We are very charitable too, and when they want sprays for

ABOVE LEFT The hall c 1970. The house had been painted white inside, but in Virginia's day the walls were pomegranate and the banisters a blue-green. The door under the stairs leads to a cellar.

OPPOSITE Taking breakfast in the kitchen, with the morning sun streaming down these worn brick steps, was one of the great pleasures of our life at Monk's House. In heavy rain, water still pours down the steps and under the kitchen door, as it did on the Woolfs' first night in the house.

funerals they come and ask us.'[7] This suggests that as well as fruit and vegetables there were flowers for cutting in the garden when they moved in. Early in 1920, Leonard was reported to be digging the flower beds and 'entirely remaking the garden'. I imagine that like anyone in possession of a new garden he spent the first year clearing, weeding, pruning and above all, making plans. Virginia helped in the garden and wrote about doing so with breathless excitement: 'Back from Monks an hour ago, after the first week end – the most perfect, I was going to say, but how can I tell what week ends we mayn't spend there? The first pure joy of the garden I mean . . .weeding all day to finish the beds in a queer sort of enthusiasm which made me say this is happiness.'[8] If this initial fervor abated, she nonetheless often helped in the garden, 'appling', weeding, dead-heading and, crucially, holding the ladder for Leonard.

By June 1921 Virginia had splashed vivid distemper on the walls of the house – pomegranate in the dining room and bright yellow in the earth closet. One of the flint-walled outbuildings, an old toolshed, had been converted into a comfortable writing room, and a laurel hedge, planted in 1882 by Jacob Verrall's sister, Caroline, cut down to give a view onto the water meadows. This hedge must have run from the end of the wall in the Orchard up to the church wall. The summer of 1921 was particularly hot and the garden parched, yet the

BELOW This 8 x 2 metre (26 x 6½ foot) wall was probably part of an old granary. Immediately to the right of this picture stood the laundry and, behind it, the earth closet, secluded behind cherry laurels. Two large cherry trees, inherited by Leonard, continued to dominate this part of the garden until the 1970s.

'... every flower that grows blows here. We have pears for breakfast'

Virginia Woolf

vegetable plot yielded peas, strawberries, beans and lettuce. It was also a time when Virginia was in the grip of another encounter with 'all the horrors of the dark cupboard of illness'[9]. She and Leonard retired to Rodmell for nearly two months, Virginia resting, reading, not keeping a diary but writing a few letters. Her third novel, the tender and experimental *Jacob's Room*, had been set aside and would not be finished until November 1921. Even in the grip of illness the garden was seductive: 'The worst of it is that the country is lovelier and lovelier. We have put brick edges to the flower beds. We have a garden room. Tell Ralph [Partridge] that every flower that grows blows here. We have pears for breakfast.'[10]

In 1922, Leonard started work on the first phase of what would become the Walled Garden, taking down the old laundry in the middle of the garden. 'Leonard is making a new flower bed, pulling down an out house, and building an earth closet. He particularly wants to know where he can buy old paving stones to make a path. Could you tell us? A place near here, if possible; because this garden too is being renovated. There's no end to his activities.'[11]

In 1923, Leonard's activities had been augmented by accepting the post of literary editor of *The Nation*, recently acquired by Maynard Keynes, and Virginia finally persuaded him that they should return to Bloomsbury after nine years in the suburbs of Richmond. By the middle of March 1924, the Woolfs and the increasingly successful Hogarth Press were installed at 52 Tavistock Square.

The way in which the Woolfs managed their finances is worth describing. Their income was pooled, household expenditure paid and any excess divided into individual 'hoards'. It seems that certain improvements were paid for

out of their hoards according to their preferences, a view supported by Virginia writing 'Having bought the Porter picture, I'm rather hard up, and yet improvements here are a great seduction . . .'[12] Virginia tended to buy furniture, rugs and paintings (she particularly liked the work of Frederick Porter and two of his paintings hang at Monk's House today), and Leonard paid for the garden and cars.

In her diary in April 1925 Virginia resolved to make £300 out of her writing to finance a bathroom and hot-water range for Monk's House. By September she heard from her publishers that *Mrs Dalloway* and *The Common Reader* 'are selling 148 & 73 weekly . . . Doesn't it portend a bathroom & a w.c . . ?'[13] By the end of 1926 Virginia's earnings outstripped Leonard's for the first time, and the longed-for bathroom and hot-water boiler were installed, affording 'the luxury of water running in torrents, boiling hot, for every conceivable purpose'.[14] Vita Sackville-West recalled visiting Monk's House and being amused by the Woolfs almost childish delight in the new flushing lavatory. Virginia and Vita had met at a dinner party in 1922, but it was not until the end of 1925 that their friendship developed into a love affair. By the June of 1926, 'the nights are long and warm; the roses flowering; and the garden full of lust and bees, mingling in the asparagus beds'.[15] Vita stayed often that summer at Monk's House, in the 'little cupboard room', Virginia taking rather more pains than she usually did for guests to ensure the room was provided for and the wine drinkable.

By the end of 1927, Virginia's fifth novel, *To the Lighthouse*, had sold well and the Woolfs were leading busy and interesting lives, divided between Rodmell and Tavistock Square, writing, editing, publishing and gardening. They bought their first car. Virginia was a hopeless driver but their enthusiasm for the joys of motoring rivalled that of Toad. The only source of discontent was the threat of development on the field lying adjacent to their northern boundary. This had been rumbling since 1921, and at one stage was so worrying they considered moving. Now, with the prospect of increased earnings and filled with ambitious plans for the garden, buying the field became a possibility. Leonard wrote to its owner, the formidably named Captain Stamper-Byng, in August 1926: 'I am particularly anxious to purchase the piece of high ground of the field running along my north wall and the churchyard wall in order to take it into my garden. I have barely an acre of land and a good deal of that is orchard and I should like to extend my gardening. I should be quite willing to buy the rest of the field in order to get the narrow strip of high ground, though, as a matter of fact, I should not use it.'[16] Negotiations were protracted, not through ill will, but through the need to resolve prior letting arrangements; eventually in 1928 Pound Croft field was bought. The Woolfs were ecstatic. 'Owning the field has given a different orient to my feelings about Rodmell. I begin to dig myself in & take part in it. And I shall build another storey to the house if I make money.'[17]

OPPOSITE ABOVE Vita Sackville-West and Virginia at the top of the lawn at Monk's House. In July 1926, Vita gave Virginia a puppy, Pinka, the golden cocker spaniel that provided the model for Flush.

OPPOSITE BELOW The bathroom in 1970. The huge roll-top bath stands at a slight slant so the water is higher on the right-hand side. T.S. Eliot noted this, and so did we. It was rather unnerving to think of the people who had lain in that bath, not least Virginia, who made a habit of rehearsing her writing out loud as she bathed each morning, not realising that Louie the cook could hear her 'talk talk talk' in the kitchen below.

ABOVE The small dining area in the hallway was once a separate room, the partition walls removed by the Woolfs. The picture above the mantelpiece is one of three paintings bought at the clearance auction. They are believed to be by and of the Glazebrook family and were among the Woolfs most treasured possessions. The portrait of Leonard to the left of the window is by Trekkie Ritchie, who donated it to the house in 1980.

'Yes, Rodmell is a perfect triumph, I consider – but L. advises me not to say so. In particular, our large combined drawing eating room, with its 5 windows, its beams down the middle, & flowers & leaves nodding in all around us.' Virginia Woolf

RIGHT Several partitions on the ground floor were removed to create this large drawing room with windows on three sides, the original spaces marked by different bricks in the floor. Virginia painted the sitting room a bright, almost viridian, green about which she was teased by her sister, the painter Vanessa Bell, and Duncan Grant. The teasing touched a nerve of insecurity in Virginia, who recognised the ease and confidence with which Vanessa created her warm domestic environment, with its painterly surfaces and, above all, children. In her diary Virginia lays out her insecurities, the sense of failure 'like a painful wave swelling about the heart . . . Oh they laughed at my taste in green paint.'[18] Green was Virginia's favourite colour and seems to have seeped into the fabric of Monk's House such that one cannot imagine the house any other colour. On sunny afternoons the plants curling around the windows, 'green-veined and quivering', cast shadows in the sunlight reflected on the walls. It is like sitting in an underwater cave. Before the extension to the north of the house was built, this was the room in which they read and smoked – Leonard a pipe; Virginia, French cigars (Petit Voltigeurs were her favourites) or hand-rolled cigarettes – ate, played the gramophone and sat in front of the fire drying their socks after long walks over the Downs.

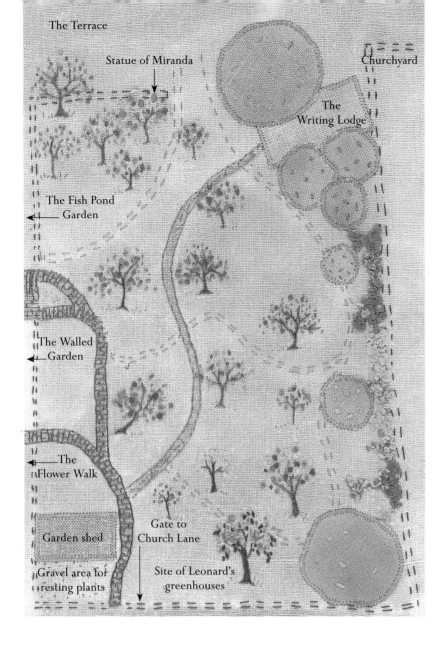

The Terrace

Statue of Miranda

Churchyard

The Writing Lodge

The Fish Pond Garden

The Walled Garden

The Flower Walk

Garden shed

Gravel area for resting plants

Gate to Church Lane

Site of Leonard's greenhouses

The Orchard

The Orchard was a huge part of the attraction of Monk's House for Leonard and Virginia and continued to be a favourite part of the garden, the 'very place to sit and talk for hours'.[1] It was certainly the part of which Virginia liked to boast, or dangle as an inducement to potential visitors such as Vita: 'there's the garden of course, all a blowing: and the orchard to sit in – which you haven't got – not with pears and apples everywhere . . .'[2]

RIGHT The Orchard, seen from the Terrace, facing south.

'*Then came the postman on this very English summer day, just the right kind of soft delicious heat and the thrushes and the blackbirds eating my apples lazily on the path – for I gathered three bushels of July pippins yesterday from an ancient apple tree ...*' Leonard Woolf

'*At moments it is divinely lovely here – hot, birds, daffodils, blue sky.*' Virginia Woolf

At Monk's House, the Orchard is the most atmospheric part of the garden, heart-stoppingly beautiful in the brief moment before the blossom is stripped from the trees by 'rough winds', satisfyingly abundant in late summer when the branches are weighed down still by bright red apples. In August 1924 Leonard wrote to Edmund Blunden: 'Then came the postman on this very English summer day, just the right kind of soft delicious heat and the thrushes and the blackbirds eating my apples lazily on the path – for I gathered three bushels of July pippins yesterday from an ancient apple tree.'[3] 'Appling' was a shared task: 'Leonard wants me to help apple picking; so I must stop, and take my seat in the heart of a tree, with pale green globes hanging round me.'[4]

One loses count of the times Virginia mentions Leonard spraying, pruning or harvesting fruit trees, often in terms of resignation as on 5 January 1927 accepting an invitation to lunch at Charleston to visit Vanessa, for herself only: 'I don't expect Leonard will leave his pruning but sends his love.'[5] Monk's House was (and still is) perishingly cold in winter, yet Leonard insisted on a visit each January to prune the fruit trees, the 'pleasantest of occupations'.[6] A novice in the first winter of 1919–20, he pruned the trees and his finger with a pruning knife given to him by Violet Dickinson, an older and close friend of Virginia's, to whom she often turned for practical advice. Even when the Ouse burst its banks and Rodmell was flooded Leonard pruned heroically in gumboots and innumerable layers of clothing. For the first couple of years at Monk's House he kept a reasonably detailed garden diary, and it is clear that fruit trees were a preoccupation. We know that, despite the yield of thirteen bushels of pears in 1919, he planted several pear cordons against the Orchard wall in 1921. On Christmas Day that year he and Virginia planted a 'Clapp's Favourite' pear tree near the gate to the Orchard. Frustratingly, the diary quickly descended into a meticulous record of purchases and yields. Surplus fruit and vegetables were sold at the Lewes Women's Institute market, and Vita Sackville-West recalls visiting Rodmell and seeing Leonard ready to cycle into Lewes with his baskets of apples and pears. The Woolfs delighted in sending presents of fruit, flowers and vegetables to friends: boxes of flowers to Vanessa when she was in London and missing her garden at Charleston, and cooking apples to Ham Spray for Lytton Strachey to enjoy with his tapioca.

In the summer of 1927 two swarms of bees settled in the Orchard. Leonard and Percy Bartholomew, their gardener for nearly twenty years, captured one of them and set up hives along the churchyard wall. By 1932, according to Percy's son Jim Bartholomew's plan of the garden (see page 191), there were four hives. Virginia took particular pleasure from the thought of produce from the garden: she bottled fruit, pickled beans, and now, a 'very bear where honey is concerned'[7], she looked forward to 'my own honey off plain bread'.[8] According to Nigel Nicolson, Vita's younger son, Virginia baked very good bread: ' . . . I knead; I stretch; I pull, plunging my hands in the warm inwards of the dough. I let the cold water stream fanwise through my fingers.'[9] In 1931 she wrote to

OPPOSITE The Orchard in spring.
ABOVE My favourite picture of Leonard and Virginia, conveying perfectly the tender closeness of their relationship.

Hugh Walpole to tell him that 'a swarm of Italian bees, that sting everybody within a mile, have made 30 lbs of wild Italian honey – some of which will be on the tea table, so come soon and eat it'.[10]

Leonard became expert at beekeeping and joined the Beekeepers' Association in his later years. Virginia liked to help with bottling the honey. Two descriptions of bees, one by Leonard and one by Virginia, are fascinating in what they reveal about the differences between their characters. In his autobiography, Leonard compared the energy in the streets of Tel Aviv to the 'busy buzz of productive ecstasy on the running board of a hive on a perfect summer day and hundreds of happy bees stream in and out of the hive on the communal business of finding nectar and storing honey.'[11] This is fine, observant writing, by someone with practical experience of handling bees; it is also the writing of someone who 'sees things so clear that he can't swim float or speculate'.[12] Whereas for Virginia, swimming, floating and above all speculation, are part of her verbal coinage – her 'romancing': 'Bees shoot whizz, like arrows of desire: fierce, sexual: weave cats cradles in the air: each whizzing from a string: the whole air full of vibration.'[13]

Marie Bartholomew, Percy's daughter, remembers Leonard bringing baskets full of apples to the village school, just over the wall, possibly in the hope of putting an end to scrumping. 'We now give them [the schoolchildren] apples, rejecting their pence, & requiring in return that they shall respect the orchard. They had already stripped several trees.'[14] So it seemed fitting to

'*There were twenty-four apple trees in the orchard, some slanting slightly, others growing straight with a rush up the trunk which spread wide into branches and formed into round red or yellow drops. Each apple-tree had sufficient space.*'

From *In the Orchard* by Virginia Woolf

RIGHT Curiously, Virginia rarely writes about the Orchard in blossom, possibly because May was a time when they often took holidays abroad. The gap in the flint wall is the entrance to the Flower Walk, and in later years Leonard created flower beds either side of this gap. These were turfed over in the early 1980s.

allow pupils from the school to plant four old Sussex varieties of apple trees in the Orchard as part of the Sussex Apple Orchard project in 2009. In 1966 Max Hastings interviewed Leonard for the London *Evening Standard* and wrote about 'a particularly rare and delicious apple' in the Orchard. The tree was in the Orchard when the Woolfs bought Monk's House and they christened it the Hesperides on account of its bright golden colour and faint pink blush. Golden apples, bestowing immortality on all who munched them, grew in Hera's garden of the Hesperides in Greek mythology. Leonard was particularly fond of this apple and wrote a folder-full of letters to experts seeking advice about suitable grafting stock. The Victoria plum tree in the Orchard has been there since Leonard's day; for the first few years of our tenancy a badger would emerge at dusk from the undergrowth behind the writing lodge to root around for the windfalls, unperturbed by human company. The proximity of the village school and the twelfth-century church of St Peter's over the Orchard walls did not always make for peace and quiet. Virginia's diaries and letters are full of irritable outbursts as bells were rung and multiplication tables chanted. At Easter each year, we organised an egg hunt in the Orchard for the school children, and I used to wonder what Virginia would have made of the children racing among the daffodils, screaming with excitement.

In 2001 the Virginia Woolf Society visited the house with Nigel Nicolson. We sat in the shade of the oldest apple tree in the Orchard and listened to a reading of Virginia's short story, 'In the Orchard', to the accompaniment of birdsong, buzzing bees, church bells and the children coming out of the school over the wall – 'continuity of living' certainly.

ABOVE LEFT Leonard in the orchard with the dogs Coco and Bess in the 1960s. Leonard planted most of the bulbs in the Orchard in the large circular beds he made beneath each tree. This allowed him to keep the grass short, which he did because he liked crocus.

ABOVE RIGHT Carpets of yellow crocuses in the Orchard seems to be a memory common to those who visited Leonard in his garden in later years. A few yellow crocuses remain, but the birds are more partial to them than to the lilac varieties, and so they tend to disappear unless replenished.

OPPOSITE My husband, Jonathan, took particular pleasure in creating the mown paths and pavements in the orchard.

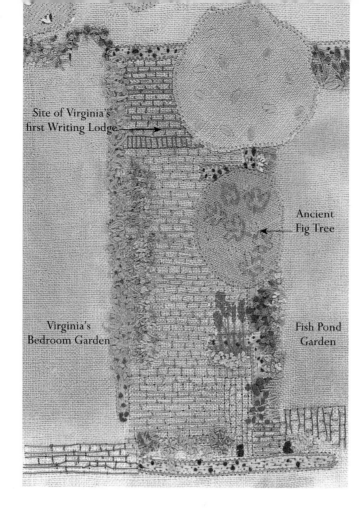

Site of Virginia's
first Writing Lodge

Ancient
Fig Tree

Virginia's
Bedroom Garden

Fish Pond
Garden

The Fig Tree Garden

The 'ancient fig tree[s]' stood in this part of the garden
long before Leonard and Virginia arrived at Monk's House.
One of the many edible presentations made by Leonard to
Trekkie Parsons, his close friend and companion from 1943
until he died, was a tin of four figs from this tree. For the first
three years of our tenancy we also enjoyed a small annual
crop and sat in its shade on hot summer days. Then a year of
unseasonal extremes induced a long period of sulking and
drooping. I suspect the tree has sulked before, for one of the
rare recorded instances of Virginia seeking garden advice
from Vita was to ask 'What is it one should do to fig trees?'[1]
Again in 1988 the National Trust garden adviser advised
cutting the fig tree to the base to encourage regrowth. We
took the same action some twenty years later and I have
confidence it will recover, though, sadly, it did not do so in
time to be photographed for this book.

RIGHT The Fig Tree Garden today, with the fig tree showing signs of recovery.

LEFT The subtle green-tinged petals of *Clematis montana* weave through the foliage of the wintersweet in summer.

ABOVE The fig tree bearing new fruits.

RIGHT The lavender in the Fig Tree Garden is Seal, an English variety known to have been available in 1929 when Leonard noted the purchase of lavender plants.

FAR RIGHT This bust to the left of Leonard was set into the wall at the entrance to the Fig Tree Garden. It seems most visitors were invited to pose, tourist-like, with their arms draped around its shoulders, and Leonard's favourite red hot pokers soaring 2 metres (6½ feet) or more above them. Interestingly, kniphofia are not mentioned in any of Leonard's notebooks although they are one of the few plants in the garden for which there is ample photographic evidence. Was it these pokers Virginia was thinking of when she placed them so erroneously in Mrs Ramsay's garden in *To the Lighthouse*?

The Fig Tree Garden is brick-floored and partially divided by low flint walls, probably the remains of piggeries. Leonard retained these walls, the brick paving and a free-standing, buttressed flint wall, 8 metres (26 feet) long and almost 2 metres (6½ feet) high, almost certainly part of the old granary, one of the three outbuildings listed in the particulars of Monk's House in 1919. I believe this area was Leonard's inspiration and starting point for laying out the rest of the central part of the garden as a series of rooms, divided by brick paths and flint walls.

At the northern end of the Fig Tree Garden, on the raised part with red bricks underfoot, stood another of the outbuildings, used by Jacob Verrall to store tools and pea props.

In 1921 Virginia wrote 'My great excitement is that we're making a beautiful garden room out of a toolhouse with a large window and a view of the downs.'[2] Leonard instructed the builders, Philcox Bros, to insert a large three-light casement window in the northern wall and to repair the existing casement window facing east to the Orchard. In warm weather it would have been an enchanting place to work, with uninterrupted views across the water meadows to Mount Caburn and the Orchard.

At that time, Pound Croft field, the land immediately in front of the north-facing window, served as the village green. Village life was observed

from the garden room: 'It is the loveliest of evenings . . . the white horse & strawberry coloured horse feeding close together; Asheham fields shorn to the colour of white corduroy; Leonard storing apples above my head & the sun coming through a pearly glass shade; so that the apples which still hang are palish red & green; the church tower a silver extinguisher rising through the trees.'[3] Noisier aspects of village life recorded by Virginia include games of stoolball and cricket, boy scouts camping in the rain, singing to keep up their spirits and, most deliciously of all, a group of young men bawling hymns from a gospel caravan. The loft above the toolshed was reached by a set of wooden steps, their feet in the next garden room. Here Leonard stored apples, occasionally irritating Virginia by stamping about, loosening the distemper from the ceiling below: 'Oh but L. will sort apples, & the little noise upsets me . . . '[4]

Imagine a Saturday morning in September 1922, and picture Virginia Woolf and Morgan Forster (who was a guest for the weekend) attempting to share the writing lodge, he working on an article, she writing a letter and 'exerci[sing] great discretion in not sneezing or knocking things over'. Clearly neither found the atmosphere conducive for Virginia claimed she 'might write a better letter if it weren't for the distinguished author, who is now scratching out every word he has written'.[5]

ABOVE FAR LEFT In the 1960s Leonard admired the hellebores in the garden of a neighbour and ordered many different species from the same supplier. These hellebores were grown by Adrian Orchard, a hellebore specialist, who knew Leonard and served with him on the committee of the Rodmell Horticultural Society.

FAR LEFT Leonard and Percy built the 'rock garden' alluded to by Virginia in 1940, on the north side of the old granary wall.

LEFT Vita Sackville-West liked the blue macropetala clematis and in a fanciful gesture we planted one to scramble through the bare branches of the *Campsis grandiflora* in spring. It was reassuring to find it mentioned in Leonard's garden notebook.

OPPOSITE The north face of the old granary wall, the shallow beds between the buttresses planted with alchemilla and self-seeding foxgloves, and a pot of the scented pelargonium 'Attar of Roses' in the foreground.

THIS PAGE The exact location of the toolshed, converted into Virginia's first garden room, with Leonard's apple loft above, was uncertain. I am grateful to Adam Nicolson, Vita's grandson, for allowing me to look through photographs at Sissinghurst to find this picture of Virginia outside the lodge. It has appeared before, in Volume 3 of the letters edited by Adam's father, Nigel. However, a cruel crop had robbed us of a clear view of the ladder to the loft which enables us to place the toolshed precisely. Later, when the Woolfs owned the field beyond, Leonard knocked down part of the flint wall and installed a tall wooden gate just beyond the steps, leading into the field. In the photograph right, Virginia is standing at the far end of the lavender bed. If you look closely at the photograph opposite, you can just make out the millstone she stands on under the Virginia creeper.

Part 3 New rooms in the garden

Orlando was published in October 1928. An 'escapade', dedicated to Vita and written in a dash over a 'singularly happy autumn' the year before, it became a best seller and the Woolfs were never again short of money. At the end of 1928 Virginia's writing brought in £1,540, double the amount of the year before, and in 1929 the figure jumped to almost £3,000. Leonard also earned money by writing (he had resigned from *The Nation* in 1925, succeeded by Edmund Blunden) and the Hogarth Press continued to be successful. The Woolfs were not extravagant. They enjoyed a comfortable lifestyle of 'ramshackle informality'. Leonard acknowledged however that 'life is easier on £3,000 a year than it is on £1,000' and the increase allowed them 'more of the things we liked to possess – books, pictures, a garden, a car'.[1] The purchase of Pound Croft field saw significant changes in the garden. They rented the lower part to a local farmer and christened the upper part 'the Terrace'. Virginia wrote: 'Leonard and I have bought a field . . . and we are making all sorts of ambitious schemes for terraces, gazebos, ponds, water lilies, fountains, carp, goldfish, statues of naked ladies and figureheads of battleships reflected in shadowy lakes.'[2]

ABOVE The creamy cup and saucer-shaped flowers of *Magnolia grandiflora* have a delicious lemony scent.
OPPOSITE Here you are standing in what used to be Pound Croft field, facing into Virginia's Bedroom Garden. This arch, now covered in wisteria, used to be a wooden gate, and Virginia's first writing lodge was immediately on the left, in the Fig Tree Garden.

Paths at Monk's House

The brick paths weaving between the flower beds, dividing the garden into rooms, are one of the most distinctive features of the garden at Monk's House. Leonard inherited the brick-paved area in the Fig Tree Garden and expanded the theme by creating various terraces, surrounded by flower beds, linked by the 'golden thread' of the paths. At the height of summer when the borders are up it is a magical mystery tour of a garden, each room hidden from the next; scented, shimmering and, to use one of Virginia's favourite words, vibrating. On a more prosaic note, they require no little maintenance: Percy's daughter Marie remembers spending hours on her hands and knees with a blunt knife scraping the weeds out of the paths. I have often wondered about the source of Leonard's inspiration as he laid out and planted the garden at Monk's House. In November 1917 he visited Garsington Manor for the first time, the home of Sir Philip and Lady Ottoline Morrell. I was struck by this passage in Lady Ottoline Morrell's memoirs: 'Yesterday as I was walking in the garden I felt so happy watching the flowers – the brown-ringed sunflowers, the red hot pokers, the phlox and montbretia, the zinnias and the marigolds, all crowd together in a gay luxurious company . . . '[3] At Garsington there was a large expanse of lawn called the terrace, a string of fish ponds, an oblong pond surrounded by yew and Italian statues, and a flower garden criss-crossed by narrow paths. Walking along these paths you are wrapped in a sense of mystery among the lushly planted 'bright dazzle'[4] of the beds. It is impossible to read these descriptions of the garden at Garsington and avoid the suspicion that memories of that garden lingered in Leonard's mind as he started to make changes to his garden at Monk's House.

RIGHT Leonard laid the millstone in the path leading from the Fig Tree Garden past the Fishpond Garden to the Orchard, surrounding it with a medley of cobbles and pavers. Virginia recalls making a cobbled path and that laying cobbles was 'rather fun'.

Plan of the paths at Monk's House

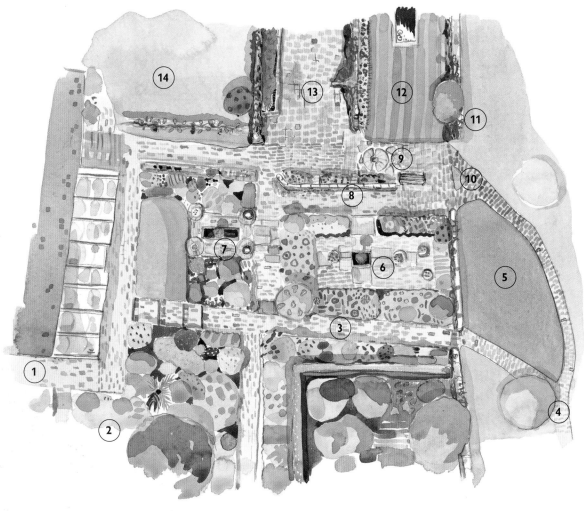

1 Path from front gate
2 The Italian Garden
3 The Flower Walk
4 Standpoint for the photograph opposite, with the Fish Pond Garden just visible through the gap in the flint walls. In 1919 this gap was filled in and a gate led to the orchard.
5 The Orchard
6 The Walled Garden
7 The Millstone Terrace
8 The old granary wall
9 Millstone and cobbles in picture, below left, the cobbles laid by Virginia and Leonard
10 The camomile triangle in the picture, centre below
11 Bench in picture, opposite
12 The Fish Pond Garden
13 The Fig Tree Garden
14 Virginia's Bedroom Garden

Walled Garden

Site of old laundry and earth closet

Rear Lawn Garden

The Millstone Terrace

In the nineteenth century Monk's House was owned by the Glazebrooks, a family of millers who also owned Rodmell Mill at the top of the down above the village. When the mill was pulled down in 1912, several millstones were hauled down to the house where Leonard and Virginia found them seven years later. Using millstones in paths was an idea pioneered by Gertrude Jekyll in her gardens, such as the one at Burgh House, which she designed in 1908. Perhaps Leonard was aware of this and had visited some of the Arts and Crafts gardens or read about them, or perhaps it simply occurred to him that using the millstones in this way was a way of absorbing the Glazebrooks into the atmosphere of the garden, again adding to the sense of 'quiet continuity'.

RIGHT Grown from seed each year these tall, shaggy zinnias created a continuous brilliant splash in the centre of the Millstone Terrace, as long as we beat the slugs.

> '*Clive & Mary came over yesterday in brilliant sun. We sat on the millstones.*' Virginia Woolf

OPPOSITE The garden in early spring, taken from the balcony of Leonard's study. It never ceased to amaze me that only a few weeks later the borders would rise so much and the view change to that on pages 12–13.
LEFT Millstones are used throughout the garden, set in the paths, thresholds and steps.
BELOW Virginia did not enjoy posing for photographs. This is an uncharacteristically posed photograph (there is a similar one featuring Leonard) and I imagine they were taken to celebrate the new Millstone Terrace. Pinka, like our cats, appreciated the warm stones as a place to bask in the sun.

Leonard was planning the new brick paths and wrote from London to Philcox Bros in Lewes: 'There are three old millstones on the path in front of the house, one laid in front of the door and two standing upright near the tap. I should like these used on the paths. The two large ones might be set in a circle in front of the door and the small one laid where the path begins after the step near the gate. I presume that the bricks will be laid level with the lawn.'[1]

The builder replied that they would wait for Mr Woolf to return from London before deciding on the final positions for the millstones. I see them in my mind's eye, pacing out the paths, deciding on the layout of the little brick terrace at the top of the lawn. Whose idea it was, finally, to set a millstone on each corner of this terrace is not related, but it was a master stroke, with the stones curving out above the lawn. Indeed it is only when you look at the photograph opposite and imagine the outbuildings in place, taking up most of the space between the wall and the pear tree just visible on the right, with everything else laid to lawn, that you appreciate Leonard's gift for garden making. We do not know how many millstones there were in the garden; it is possible there were more or perhaps the builder suggested buying more. They are a *leitmotif* in the garden paths, their pale ribbed circles like ammonites in rocks.

The Millstone Terrace was a comfortable spot to sit in the garden, perched on the edge of the millstones, leaning back against the large terracotta olive oil jars. Imagine a 'blazing hot day' with Virginia sitting on the warm millstone, 'trying to read a manuscript when a battered old woman carrying a satchel of shiny books appeared, and asked me if I believed in God, because if I did I must buy her books, and if I did not, still more must I buy her books. So we began to argue about God and the soul and Leonard only throwing twigs at me from the cherry tree which he was scraping of ivy. . .'[2] How I would have liked to eavesdrop on that conversation. The poor old woman was rescued by the, possibly divine, intervention of a delivery for Virginia and scarpered.

'. . . the garden is full of zinnias. The zinnias are full of slugs. L goes out at night with a lantern and collects snails, which I hear him cracking . . .'

Virginia Woolf

LEFT The provenance of the large terracotta jars is, frustratingly, unknown. They appear in the earliest photographs of the garden. On her first visit Virginia noticed 'a large earthen pot . . . where the path strikes off, crowned with a tuft of purple samphire. One pot, not two.'[3] We took as our inspiration instead *To the Lighthouse* and Mr Ramsay 'seeing again the urns with the trailing red geraniums'.

OPPOSITE Leonard was very fond of zinnias. The combination of soft lilac blue and burnt orange appears often in Vanessa Bell's paintings, and indeed in a delectable gouache by Angelica Garnett that stands on the mantelpiece in Virginia's bedroom and inspired the palette for much of the planting in the garden (see page 97). Here it is represented by *Perovskia* 'Blue Spire', self-sown campanula and crocosmia (referred to often by Virginia by its old-fashioned name of montbretia).

The Terrace

Fig Tree Garden

The Orchard

The Fish Pond Garden

Leonard had 'a passion for ponds'[1] and the first area of the garden to change following the purchase of Pound Croft field was the area adjacent to the Fig Tree Garden, into the middle of which he set a deep rectangular pond. This narrow strip of south-facing garden, enclosed on three sides by flint walls, enjoyed views into the Orchard. Before the new writing room with its brick terrace was built, the Fish Pond Garden was where the Woolfs gathered with guests, lying on rugs on the grass or lolling in rickety canvas chairs.

RIGHT For spring we planted the same mix of tulips each year, Esther, Negrita and Queen of Night, in the hope that they would flower at the same time as the magnolia. In the summer the colour palette is quite different: a row of hardy fuchsias, interspersed with deep pink hollyhocks lines the wall with the busts.

OPPOSITE, CLOCKWISE FROM TOP LEFT *Magnolia* x *soulangeana* 'Lennei'; the pasque flower, which we grew as much for its fluffy seedheads as the bright anemone-like flowers; *Viola* 'Coeur d'Alsace', ordered by Leonard in 1954; these mysteriously beautiful iris flower near Virginia's bust.
ABOVE RIGHT Morgan Forster, Leonard, and the rusty saw, taken by Virginia outside the old tool shed on 7 April 1934.
ABOVE FAR RIGHT Angelica Bell, Julian Bell and Lettice Ramsey in the Fish Pond Garden. When the Monk's House albums were published online, Woolf enthusiasts were able to browse through Leonard and Virginia's photograph albums. Coming across this picture was a moment of great excitement, for there was the old writing lodge, its eastern elevation standing in the gap now filled by a large magnolia.

Virginia seemed to feel ambivalent about entertaining at Rodmell. A day of visitors was a day without peace, and without peace there was no work. 'The truth is I like it when people actually come but I love it when they go,'[2] Virginia confided in her diary. Often she wanted them to go as soon as they arrived. Morgan Forster, always rather nervous around Virginia, despite his close and abiding friendship with Leonard, described in a letter to Christopher Isherwood a hideous weekend in which 'I was much irritated at being left so much to myself. Here are Woolfs who read – Leonard the *Observer* and Virginia *The Sunday Times* and then retired in literary studies to write till lunch. At least L has just come out but I, piqued, continue my letter to you and he, most displeased cuts the deadwood out of a buddleia with a small rusty saw. Virginia has now suggested a photograph should be taken of me. Leonard thinks it's a good idea and continues to saw the buddleia. It is five minutes to one, no one . . . the bell rings and I must jolly well lock up this letter during lunch or it will get read.'[3] We can assume lunch was good: Morgan Forster wrote years later that Virginia not only knew how to describe good food, but also provided it at her table.

The toolshed overlooked the Fish Pond Garden and it is probably from here that Viginia looked up from her writing and observed Leonard planting hollyhocks, or Leonard and Percy Bartholomew installing the conduit pipe for the 'chocolate brown'[4] pond. 'It is a fine hot day, and I am sitting in my garden room which has a fine view of the downs and marshes and an oblique view of Leonard's fish pond, in which it is our passion to observe the gold fish. There should be four, and one carp; but it is the rarest event to see them all together – and yet I can assure you that so to see them matters more to us both than all that is said at the Hague.'[5]

The lily pond makes an appearance in Virginia's last novel, *Between the Acts*: 'Lucy still gazed at the lily pool. "All gone", she murmured, "under the leaves". Scared by shadows passing the fish had withdrawn. She gazed at the water. Perfunctorily she caressed her cross. But her eyes went water searching, looking for fish. The lilies were shutting; the red lily, the white lily, each on its plate of leaf.'

'Leonard's fish pond, in which it is our passion to observe the gold fish.'
Virginia Woolf

The planting in the Fish Pond Garden was and is still confined to narrow, chalk-filled beds beneath the flint walls. The soil is poor, dry and unrewarding, the worst in the garden. In the garden plan of 1932 (see page 191) there are three fruit trees marked against the northern wall. Now there is only a fig tree in the north-east corner, and a beautiful *Magnolia* x *soulangeana* 'Lennei' planted next to the Stephen Tomlin bronze bust of Virginia. Sitting for 'thrush like' Tomlin was not a happy experience for either of them. Fond of him though she was, Virginia was averse to being looked at. She felt pinned down, 'like a piece of whalebone bent'.[6] Leonard later recalled that she got into 'such a stew about it' that he thought it would make her ill. It must have been frustrating for Tomlin when Leonard asked him to stop and the bust was left unfinished.

ABOVE LEFT Leonard loved this fishpond and there are a number of photographs of him gazing into its depths, sometimes feeding the fish from an old toffee tin.
ABOVE Virginia with writer John Lehmann, her nephew Julian's best friend, at Monk's House in the early 1930s. He had joined the Hogarth Press as a trainee manager, but left after a year or so to travel. Later he returned, eventually buying Virginia's share of the partnership in 1938.

RIGHT AND BELOW The
Fish Pond Garden, facing south.
Years later, after Virginia's
death, Leonard wrote to
Trekkie Parsons: 'When I got
back here tonight, I did wish you
were with me to see the pond
covered with the blood red &
the cream waterlilies & bright
blue sky reflected in it . . . '[7]

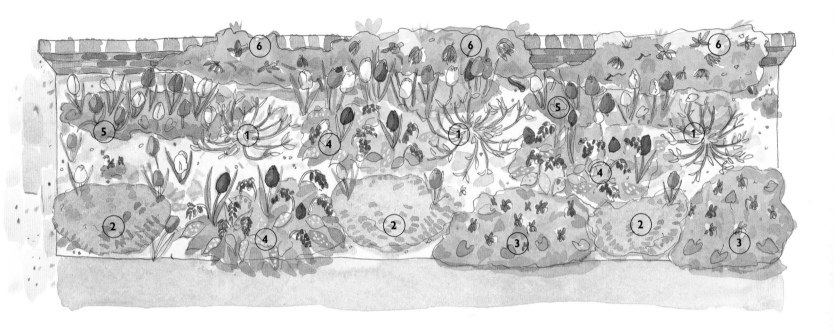

Spring tulip planting plan

This simple planting plan is inspired by that particularly lovely combination of blue and pink found in the flowers of pulmonaria. I had in mind the difficult narrow border lying beneath the 1-metre (3 foot) high flint wall bearing the busts of Leonard and Virginia. It faces east, and the soil is dry, chalky and poor.

We planted a mix of three colours of single late-flowering tulips to coincide with the flowering of the magnolia. Three hardy *Fuchsia magellanica* bushes spring forth in summer, with large clumps of *Nepeta racemosa* 'Walker's Low' between. For this plan I have added *Epimedium grandiflorum* 'Lilafee' along the base of the wall, the heart-shaped leaves and delicate purple flowers providing a perfect foil for the tulips. You could add a sprinkling of *Allium cernuum*, a delicate allium with a shower head of pink bells in spring. They need to grow through things so that they are supported and their unsightly foliage is hidden as they die off. Then, when the fuchsias and nepeta take over, the epimediums, pulmonarias and violas hang about happily in shade.

The two blue *Viola odorata* grown by Leonard were 'Governor Herrick' (a hybrid) and 'Princess of Wales', both rare. Together with *Pulmonaria* 'Blue Ensign', violas provide a colourful base for the mix of Esther, Negrita and dark Queen of Night tulips. How many bulbs you use depends on the effect you want. I prefer them dotted in clumps rather than massed (for which the recommended number is a shocking 70 per square metre/11 square feet), and it is worth separating a few from the mix to use under different plants – Queen of Night under the *Pulmonaria* 'Blue Ensign' for example. You could also dot some aquilegias in the gaps for that difficult moment at the end of spring when summer has not quite arrived. We did not lift our tulips; we left them in and planted more each year.

1   *Fuchsia magellanica* 'Versicolor'
2   *Nepeta racemosa* 'Walker's Low'
3   *Viola odorata* 'Intense Blue'
4   *Pulmonaria* 'Blue Ensign' (save some Esther tulips to plant under these)
5   *Epimedium grandiflorum* 'Lilafee', underplanted with tulips and perhaps also *Allium cernuum*
6   *Clematis montana* 'Marjorie'

Underplanting of tulips
Negrita x 100
Queen of Night x 75
Esther x 100

OPPOSITE CLOCKWISE FROM TOP LEFT
Esther and Queen of Night tulips. Pulmonaria: we inherited and divided this variety. *Clematis montana* 'Marjorie'. *Viola odorata*, Queen of Night tulips and *Muscari* 'Valerie Finnis'.

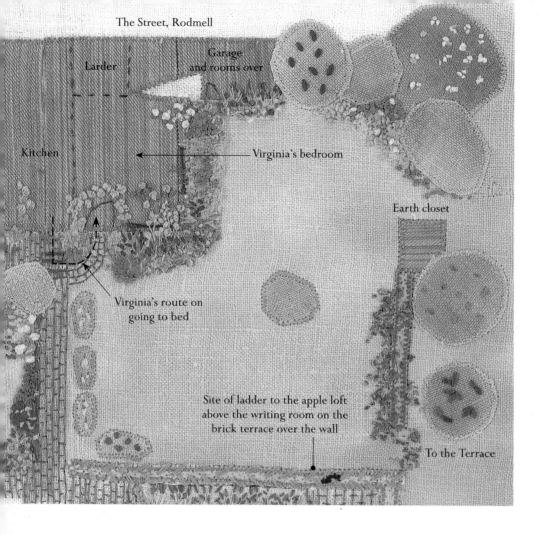

The Street, Rodmell

Larder

Garage and rooms over

Kitchen

Virginia's bedroom

Earth closet

Virginia's route on going to bed

Site of ladder to the apple loft above the writing room on the brick terrace over the wall

To the Terrace

Virginia's Bedroom Garden

In 1929, while Leonard was absorbed in his new schemes for the garden after the purchase of Pound Croft field, Virginia planned her new rooms. The year had started with a visit to Berlin to see Vita and Harold Nicolson in the company of Duncan Grant, Vanessa and Quentin Bell. As a result of 'Berlin racketing' and an adverse reaction to the veronal Vanessa gave her for seasickness on the return journey, Virginia arrived home very ill and spent several weeks in bed on 'stiff tumblers of bromide', allowed to see no one. By the end of March she was feeling better and determined to finish off *Phases of Fiction* to clear her mind ready to start a 'new imaginative book'.[1] Planning a new room in which to work was a priority: 'I have money to build it, money to furnish it.'[2]

RIGHT The rose around the window is Princesse Marie, an old rose that I found at Heale House Gardens. It is not a repeat flowering rose so *Clematis* 'Madame Julia Correvon' provides colour later in the season, with lavender, penstemon, campanula and, later, asters.

RIGHT The view from the door of Virginia's bedroom 'where the pears are'. Replanted by us in 2001 they are Beurré Hardy and Williams' Bon Chrétien, both varieties grown by Leonard.
OPPOSITE The tiled fireplace surround is by Vanessa Bell, featuring a lighthouse, a little cutter with blood-red sails and delicate smudges of Virginia's green. '2lbs of green paint' were ordered for this room in 1929. The curtains are a reproduction of 'Grapes', a fabric designed by Duncan Grant in 1932.
BELOW 'It is shameful that I haven't answered you or thanked you for the lovely green shell. This has become part of my washing table at Rodmell – a glorified soap dish.'[3] (letter to Ottoline Morrell).

'a lovely wonderful room . . . just what I've always hoped for' Virginia Woolf

The new book hovering was to be *The Waves*, although the original title was *The Moths*, inspired by a letter from Vanessa at Cassis describing the flutter of enormous moths flying around her lamp. Writing in the toolshed had become impossible in cold weather, even wrapped in a blanket. 'Philcox came out and drew a sketch of two rooms in a jiffy; so I await result; and tremble with excitement . . .' The top floor was to be her bedroom and the ground floor a room in which to write. 'They're to be built on next to the kitchen where the pears are – of brick, I think, painted white.'[4]

Correspondence with the builder reveals that there were several fruit trees and at least one had to be sacrificed in order to build the extension. Work started in 1929 and took longer to complete than expected, with the rooms being ready in December of that year. I imagine them climbing for the first time the narrow matchboard-enclosed staircase to the top floor and emerging into the light, warm room with its view across the garden to the water meadows.

LEFT AND OPPOSITE During a period of illness in 1936 Virginia wrote to Morgan Forster telling him she was 'rebinding all my Shakespeares – 29 vols – in coloured paper, and thinking of then reading one of them'.[5] Virginia had learned book binding before her marriage. It is possible that she also marbled these papers as this was something she enjoyed doing and taught the village schoolchildren to do during the war. These bound volumes of Shakespeare were recently returned to Monk's House. Unpacking the boxes, I could not resist brushing my bare thumb gently over her distinctive writing on the spine labels, before arranging them in a painted bookcase.

BELOW LEFT Queen of Night tulips, bluebells, comfrey and sprays of *Syringa pubescens* ssp. *microphylla* 'Superba' in a French glazed jug.

We know from Louie Mayer (née Everest), the Woolfs' cook from 1934, that Leonard brought Virginia her breakfast on a tray every morning and would sit on her bed while they talked. Not hard then to imagine them gazing out at the view and agreeing that it was the best room in the house and a pity to waste it on a bedroom, even for someone who spent more time than most ill in bed. 'We have a project of making my bedroom the sitting room – for the view; to let it waste, day after day, seems a crime: elderly eyes cannot waste.'[6] Leonard and Percy swapped the furniture around and the ground floor became her bedroom, giving rise to innumerable academic theories about Woolf and the symbolism of her 'solitary chamber'. Anyone looking at the house would quickly appreciate that creating internal access to the new ground floor room was impossible and that Virginia had decided to sacrifice convenience (in both senses of the word) in order to enjoy using the top floor as an indoor writing room and sitting room they could share in the evenings. By September 1930, the weather was cold and wet 'but we have our new sitting room and a roaring log fire and so are very snug. Leonard's garden really has been a miracle – vast white lilies, and such a blaze of dahlias that even today one feels lit up.'[7]

When the toolshed was too cold, Virginia wrote in the new upstairs sitting room. If she was unwell, she would work in the bedroom below, sitting in a

OPPOSITE The lawned area in front of Virginia's bedroom looked completely different in 1919 when it was Jacob Verrall's main vegetable garden, where 'cabbages merged into roses'. Behind the cordon apple tree a rolled ash path led off to the left, to the tall wooden gate leading onto the Terrace. After the purchase of Pound Croft field Leonard created a new kitchen garden in the north-east corner of the garden, but kept the fruit trees and established asparagus beds here. The lawned area was surrounded by espaliered and cordoned fruit trees trained on wires supported by metal posts. In the middle were beds filled with vegetables, flowers for cutting and the precious asparagus. This arrangement persisted into the 1960s. ABOVE RIGHT The view from the new top-floor room in 1933. Cordoned fruit trees are ranged along the flint wall which is now draped in wisteria (see next page). The two elm trees, christened Leonard and Virginia by the Woolfs, stood in the lower part of Pound Croft field but rose up over the Terrace, their interlacing branches an instantly recognisable lodestar in even the most faded archive photograph.

chair with wooden arms, across which she laid a board to which she had glued an inkwell. She would move the chair around to enjoy different views of the garden – the red hot pokers and the sun rising on the apples 'winking in the trees' or the asparagus beds. Privacy was occasionally a problem: 'I sleep and dress in full view of the garden.'[8]

By now, Virginia was deep into writing *The Waves* and in the first throes of an intense friendship with Ethel Smyth, the composer and suffragette, some ten years older than Virginia, who had written to Virginia after reading *A Room of One's Own*. Louie remembered that Ethel would arrive at Monk's House 'in her funny old car, get out and stand at the gate, yelling at the top of her voice for Virginia'.[9] Ethel wrote to Virginia nearly every day, sometimes twice, with supplementary telegrams.

Unsurprisingly, Leonard was not as taken with Ethel who, though clever, was loud, opinionated (she and Virginia argued often in letters), domineering and militant. 'No, no no!' was Leonard's pained reaction to Virginia proposing a stay in Woking with Ethel. Ethel was in love with Virginia, and Virginia deeply fond, loyal and not above flirting (at least in letters), but not in love. It is tempting to suggest that the combination of the age difference and Ethel's untramelled frankness led Virginia to treat her, unconsciously, as a therapist in whom she confided about episodes of her life in a way she had never done before.

'In the garden where the trees stood thick over flowerbeds, ponds and greenhouses, the birds sang in the hot sunshine, each alone.' *The Waves*, Virginia Woolf

RIGHT A wisteria has run rampant along the tall flint wall to the north, taking no prisoners in its path. The archway to the Terrace is where there was once a tall wooden gate, and the foot of the ladder to the apple loft above Virginia's first writing lodge stood roughly where the clump of daffodil foliage is, bottom right.

'Madness is terrific . . . and in its lava I still find most of the things I write about.'[10] There was also a mutual intellectual respect and a shared fury at a world organised and run by men. Their exchanges on this subject came into play in two of Virginia's later books, *The Years* and *Three Guineas*.

The painterly interludes in *The Waves*, describing the passage of the sun over the sea from dawn until dusk, illuminating a garden, are filled with echoes of the distinctive sounds of the garden at Monk's House and the sound of the sea at Talland House, the Stephen family's home in St Ives, Cornwall. Virginia wrote later that her memories of the garden at Talland House were somehow 'more real than the present moment'.[11] In *Moments of Being* she admitted that even as she looked at the garden at Monk's House, she saw it always through the prism of her memories of the one at Talland House. 'In the garden where the trees stood thick over flowerbeds, ponds and greenhouses, the birds sang in the hot sunshine, each alone.' The musician in me cannot help wondering whether Virginia's friendship with Ethel and their discussions about music influenced the rhythm of the nine interludes. In her diary Virginia wrote, 'She [Ethel] says writing music is like writing novels. One thinks of the sea – naturally one gets a phrase for it. Orchestration is colouring.'[12]

Although Virginia suffered from several bouts of ill health in 1930, it was one of her happiest years. Her diaries bear witness to the rich creative process of writing *The Waves*, her friendship with Vita continued to be close – she spent time at Long Barn and went to view the newly acquired Sissinghurst – and Ethel bombarded her with interesting letters. Nellie Boxall, their cook, with whom relations had become unbearably fraught, was dispatched to Tavistock Square, leaving them with Annie Thompsett, 'another of those plums . . . dropped into our hands'[13], in charge of the kitchen at Monk's House and living out in one of a pair of cottages Leonard had bought in the village. Life without Nellie's moods and recriminations felt as good as removing tight shoes from hot, swollen feet. The summer was the 'comfortablest', indeed 'the happiest summer since we had Monk's House; the most satisfactory'.'But O – again – how happy I am: how calm, for the moment how sweet life is with L. here, in its regularity & order, & the garden & the room at night & music & my walks & writing easily & interestedly.'[14]

Virginia's bedroom garden plan

This garden plan is inspired by the border outside Virginia's bedroom, adapted to be useful for a bed that wraps around the corner of a house with one limb facing north. The plants here can be supplemented with spring bulbs, forget-me-nots and deep pink wallflowers, followed by alliums.

The pair of climbing roses forms the backdrop to this plan, with *Clematis montana* 'Marjorie' for the early summer and *Clematis* 'Madame Julia Correvon' for later on. The fennel is a nod to the way cabbages merge into roses at Monk's House. 'Charles de Mills' rose is a favourite and prefers to have a little respite from the sun, otherwise its blooms fade within the day.

OPPOSITE Main picture, *Clematis* 'Madame Julia Correvon'. Top, *Geranium* 'Ann Folkard' with *Papaver orientale* 'Karine'. Centre, Penstemon 'Claret' with *Allium sphaerocephalon*. Bottom, *Rosa* 'Charles de Mills'.

1 *Lavandula angustifolia* 'Munstead'
2 *Salvia sclarea* (clary sage)
3 Penstemon 'Claret'
4 *Campanula lactiflora* 'Loddon Anna'
5 *Geranium* 'Ann Folkard'
6 *Perovskia* (Russian sage)
7 Lupins
8 Fennel
9 *Papaver orientale* 'Karine'
10 *Rosa* 'Princesse Marie'
11 *Clematis* 'Madame Julia Correvon'

12 *Clematis montana* 'Marjorie'
13 *Rosa* 'Madame Alfred Carrière'
14 *Rosa* 'Charles de Mills'
15 Japanese anemones
16 *Astrantia major*
17 White phlox
18 *Hydrangea macrophylla* 'Blue Wave'
19 *Chaenomeles speciosa* 'Nivalis' (white flowering quince)
20 *Buxus*

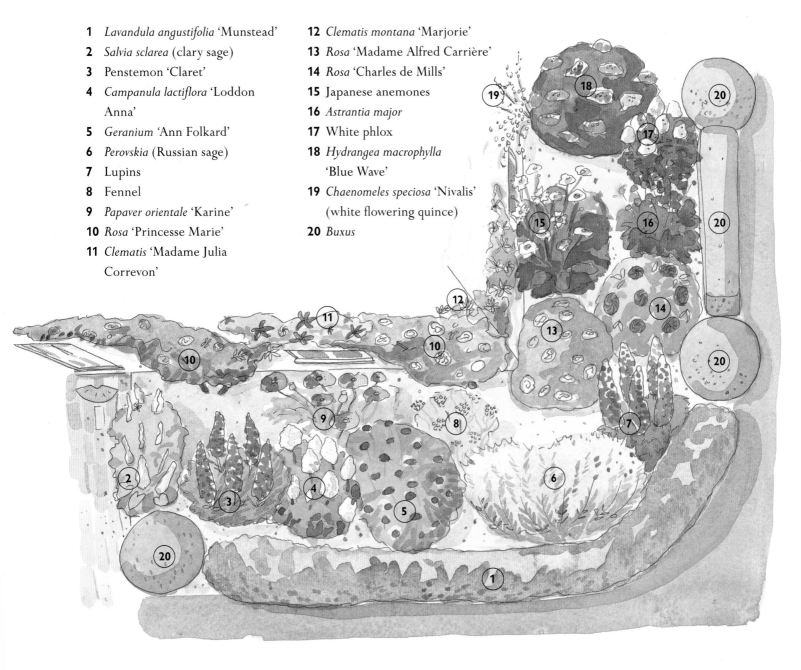

Leonard's Roses

Leonard loved roses, although he despised floribundas. Looking through the ones he ordered and liked, all of these would, I think, be acceptable.

LEFT Paul's Himalayan Musk
ABOVE Fantin-Latour
OPPOSITE, CLOCKWISE FROM
TOP LEFT Falstaff; Cecile Brunner
(the shrub, not the climber);
Moonlight; Charles de Mills.

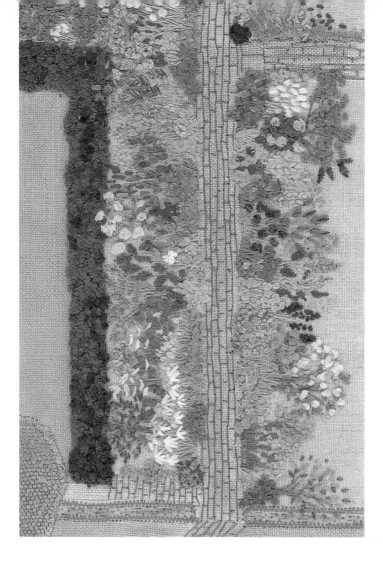

The Flower Walk

The Flower Walk comprises the two borders on either side of the long brick path running west to east from the top of the steps by the lawn to the Orchard. The southern border is 1.5 metres (5 feet) deep and set against a tall yew hedge. Opposite, the border is the southern side of a long border 3 metres (10 feet) deep. In 1919, the whole of the southern border in front of the yew hedge was laid to lawn and the brick path did not exist. The instinct is to treat this Flower Walk as a double border, and yet the conditions on either side are quite different. The yew hedge acts effectively as a northern wall, casting the border on the south into shade for most of the day, whereas opposite, the border bathes in the sun for several hours each day.

RIGHT The Flower Walk, facing the house.

FAR LEFT A rose supported by a stout tripod, underplanted with *Geranium psilostemon*.
LEFT A mixed clump of delphiniums, including an azure delphinium from Margery Fish's garden at East Lambrook Manor.
OPPOSITE The Flower Walk facing the Orchard. The English irises front right were on Leonard's plant list.

There is very little evidence about the creation of these borders or precisely what was planted in them. A minute of grainy black and white footage of a BBC documentary made by Stephen Peet in 1967 shows Leonard and broadcaster Malcolm Muggeridge strolling through the Orchard and turning into the Flower Walk at the Orchard end. Leonard had flower beds on the Orchard side of the flint wall dividing the garden and Orchard, and beyond one can see that the planting is mixed, tall and lush.

Leonard recorded every single plant he bought, but rarely where he planted them. Virginia's diaries and letters throw out odd hints, but they relate to the earlier years at Monk's House when his plants tended to be more commonplace: dahlias, carnations, pinks, wallflowers, asters. One extract from a letter from Virginia gives a clue to the planting style: 'Our garden is a perfect variegated chintz: asters, plumasters, zinnias, geums, nasturtiums & so on: all bright, cut from coloured papers, stiff, upstanding as flowers should be.'[1]

A common memory of the garden is that Leonard's flowers were 'vast', 'gigantic', and 'seemed to grow larger for him than for than anyone else'. 'The garden is at is finest: the big bed spread with brilliant flowers, their petals almost touching.'[2] There is magic in the soil at Monk's House. Or perhaps it was Percy's regular emptying of the contents of the cesspool over the garden.

In his later years, Leonard developed a taste for more unusual species, particularly bulbs. He also also liked to raise flowers in his glasshouse – we know he had great success with freesias and carnations and grew cinerarias and gloxinias for the house. The National Trust lease listed several plants which we should try to use. With one exception these were orange. It seems that the

fact Leonard was known to have liked red hot pokers and grew brightly coloured plants in his glasshouses meant that he only liked brightly coloured flowers in the garden. However, there is ample evidence in his garden notebooks that he also favoured purple, pinky purple and white flowers. This is borne out by a quotation from Virginia's diaries: 'Never has the garden been so lovely – all ablaze even now; dazzling one's eyes with reds & pinks & purples & mauves; the carnations in great bunches, the roses lit like lamps.'[3]

Was Virginia a gardener? In 1907 she spent a summer in Rye with her older brother Adrian: '...we have a real country cottage ... and a garden, and an orchard; I don't really enjoy any of these things; it bores me dreadfully to cut the flowers.'[4] Yet the rapture with which she writes about the garden of her childhood holiday home in St Ives leaves no doubt that she enjoyed gardens and found them inspiring. However, I do not think she was particularly interested in garden making; after all, she was the lover and intimate friend of one of the most exciting gardeners of the century and yet hardly exchanged a word on the subject in nearly twenty years of regular correspondence. Such mentions as there were made it clear that she was neither knowledgeable nor technically skilled. Perhaps she felt unequal to a conversation about horticulture with Vita, who refused on one occasion to trust her with a gift of plants for Leonard for fear they would die through Virginia's neglect. If she had opinions about how the garden should be laid out there is no evidence of it in her letters or diaries. Instead she took pleasure in boasting about the garden being 'all Leonard's doing'[5], and enjoyed helping him when required.

It is curious that Leonard did not proffer editorial advice about the way in which Virginia writes about flowers in her novels. Was this perhaps because he knew that Virginia was at her most vulnerable as she finished her books and handed them over to be read for the first time? It cannot help but raise the question how the world of literature might have been different had all of her writings been subject to the red pen of an objective and, almost certainly, male editor. In a letter to Lytton Strachey shortly after the publication of *Night and Day* in October 1919 Virginia asks him to 'tell Carrington I went into the question of the roses with some care'.[6] The description of Mary and Elizabeth Datchet 'cutting roses ... and laying them, head by head, in a shallow basket' in a Lincolnshire garden in December was met with incredulity not only by Carrington but by the reviewer for *The Times*. The American publishers asked Virginia to correct any mistakes and she sought the advice of her close friend, Violet Dickinson, pointing out that there were certainly long-stemmed pink roses at Kew in December. The passage remained unchanged. When *To the Lighthouse* was published Virginia recalled a critic writing that her 'horticulture and natural history is in every instance wrong: there are no rooks, elms or dahlias in the Hebrides; my sparrows are wrong and so are my carnations'.[7] She was not particularly bothered by the criticism, and indeed poked fun at her own lack of knowledge, as in this letter of 1937: 'if only I could remember the names of flowers, and what Leonard is proud of this summer, it would be like one of old Miss Jekyll's letters, minus the common sense.'[8]

OPPOSITE ABOVE *Clematis viticella* cheers up a *Vibernum opulus* in summer.
OPPOSITE BELOW *Astrantia* 'Roma' and lavender. Astrantia is such a useful, well-behaved perennial, equally happy in shady spots.
LEFT *Campanula lactiflora* 'Pritchard's Variety', *Geranium* 'Ann Folkard' and rose Fantin-Latour.
ABOVE Clary sage and nigella grown from seed each year.

'never has the garden been so lovely . . . dazzling one's eyes with reds & pinks & purples & mauves'

Virginia Woolf

RIGHT '. . . crossing the garden by the pale flowers.' *Echinacea purpurea* 'Alba' and *Cosmos* 'Purity' in the flower walk. Leonard liked white flowers – further along this border is a large clump of white Japanese anemones. Each year we grew large amounts of cosmos, white and deep pink, as it is such a useful filler for beds, flowering until the first frosts. It is easy to grow and tolerates any soil and aspect. 'Purity' does need some support.

A corner 'in the spirit of Bloomsbury'

It was suggested by the Natonal Trust that we garden 'in the spirit of Bloomsbury', using bright colours in a painterly style. So we were surprised to discover, during our first summer at Monk's House, that *Phlox paniculata* 'Alba' had elbowed its way through the central bed that on one side forms half of the Flower Walk, and on the other edges one side of the Walled Garden. Standing in the bed that summer was like standing in the foam of a very large breaking wave. We dug it out of the bed and redistributed some of it around the shadier corners of the garden where I think it does its best work, underplanted with comfrey, its tidy green shoots in spring a good foil for bulbs. We now had a very large empty space to fill and this plan is inspired by a corner of a bed some 12 metres (40 feet) long. The little painting by Angelica Garnett (opposite) inspired the chalky blues and purples of nigella, *Campanula lactiflora* 'Pritchard's Variety' and *Nepeta racemosa* 'Walker's Low' set against the burnt orange of the *Hemerocallis fulva*, zinnias and tithonia, with touches of bright pink.

Our knowledgeable volunteer gardener, Janet, a retired social worker, who came on Wednesday mornings carrying a tidy basket of tools, suggested *Rosa chinensis* 'Mutabilis'. Its bronze leaves and curling, pink-tinged stems required it to be placed behind an inherited clump of *Euphorbia griffithii* 'Fireglow'. For spring we underplanted the euphorbia with tulips – Ballerina and Queen of Night – and *Fritillaria imperialis* 'Aurora' – burnt-orange crown imperials. Yes, they smell of fox, but Leonard loved them. The *Rosa chinensis* 'Mutabilis' is a wonderful backdrop for bronze-leafed plants in summer or even the deep red buds of perennial geraniums as they break through the ground in spring. It flowers for months and the foliage works well in autumnal flower arrangements, the tiny deep pink buds opening to pale apricot flowers, which deepen again to pink as they age. It needs good support. Crocosmia – the old-fashioned, orange variety which was known by Virginia as montbretia – and hemerocallis earn their keep by providing vibrant upstanding foliage and good seedheads for the autumn, particularly crocosmia.

I tried to mix up the colours the way it seems Leonard liked to do, rather than creating large clumps. So we threaded *Verbena bonariensis* between the groups of plants or mixed it with the tall annuals, such as *Tithonia rotundifolia*. In each bed we kept certain areas clear of summer perennials, planting spring bulbs among blue and white pulmonarias, violets or wallflowers and adding annuals (grown under glass) once the spring bulbs had died back: tithonia, zinnias and nigella.

LEFT FROM TOP *Rosa chinensis* 'Mutabilis'. *Persicaria amplexicaulis* 'Firetail'. Crocosmia 'Lucifer' against *Veronicastrum virginicum* 'Fascination' and *Campanula lactiflora* 'Pritchard's Variety'. *Hemerocallis fulva* and *Nepeta racemosa* 'Walker's Low'.

1 *Hemerocallis fulva* (or common orange day lily)
2 *Euphorbia griffithii* 'Fireglow'
3 *Geranium* 'Ann Folkard'
4 *Nepeta racemosa* 'Walker's Low'
5 Zinnias
6 *Alchemilla mollis*
7 Nigella
8 *Campanula lactiflora* 'Pritchard's Variety'
9 *Rosa chinensis* 'Mutabilis'
10 *Crocosmia* 'Lucifer'
11 *Verbena bonariensis*
12 *Echinacea purpurea*
13 *Aconitum* 'Sparks Variety'
14 *Veronicastrum Virginicum* 'Pink Glow'
15 *Buddleja davidii* 'Black Knight'
16 *Tithonia rotundifolia*
17 *Veronicastrum virginicum* 'Fascination'
18 Pear tree
19 *Persicaria amplexicaulis* 'Firetail'

'Our garden is a perfect variegated chintz . . . asters, plumasters, zinnias, geums, nasturtiums . . . all bright, stiff, upstanding, cut from brightly coloured paper as flowers should be.'
Virginia Woolf

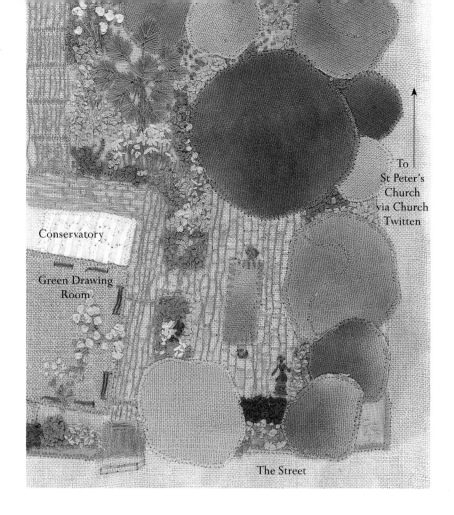

Conservatory

Green Drawing
Room

To
St Peter's
Church
via Church
Twitten

The Street

The Italian Garden

The 1919 conveyance of Monk's House did not include a
small strip in the south-west corner of the plot, immediately
on the right as one walks through the gate. This strip once
faced on to Church Lane, the narrow path leading to St
Peter's Church, and had been the site of a tiny parsonage
attached to Monk's House which was demolished in 1856.
This explains why the first 70 metres (230 feet) or so of the
boundary with Church Lane consists of close-board fencing
rather than the flint wall, which continues up to the lych gate.
In 1920 Leonard bought this small strip, laying it to lawn and
taking the area of his garden from three-quarters of an acre to
one acre precisely, as it had been in 1350, when the gift of the
parsonage was made for 'a messuage and an acre of land for
a habitation for the parson of Radmelde for ever'.

RIGHT The Italian Garden, seen from the step by the gate. This was the site of a small parsonage
until 1856.

RIGHT The shepherdess from the grocer's shop in Barcombe. Her missing hands and forearm are neatly wrapped in tissue paper in a drawer.
OPPOSITE Over the years we experimented with different planting for the urns but finally settled on *Muscari armeniacum* 'Valerie Finnis', with its pale grey-blue flowers, so much more subtle than the brighter blue varieties. One year, a little perennial geranium appeared in one of the urns and as it seemed to work quite well, I divided it and grew the muscari through it – muscari is always better growing through something which disguises the untidy foliage. The geranium, which closely resembles and might be *Geranium macrorrhizum* 'Bevan's Variety' was past its best by July when we replaced everything with the delicate white pelargonium Lilian Pottinger, with apple-scented leaves. The muscari and perennial geranium had a rest on the gravel by the shed, to be brought back in the autumn.
BELOW In archive pictures this pot appears, planted with a hydrangea. We chose Ayesha, which was first released after the Second World War.

'We've made another pond too. At first the water slanted up one way and down another. And now where can I buy pots, Italian, and a statue? That's my contribution to the garden.' Virginia Woolf

In May 1933, having acquired a new car ('silver and green . . . it glides with the smoothness of eel, with the speed of a swift'[1]) the Woolfs set off on a motoring holiday through France to Tuscany. This Italian holiday made a profound impression on both of them and Virginia's letters reveal her to be intoxicated by Tuscany, 'every tree flowering, every bird singing'.[2] In September she wrote in her diary: 'L. is having the new pond made, the old one re-grouted, & is going to pave the front garden. *Flush*, I think with some pleasure has made these extravagances possible.'[3] The following week: 'L's new pond & garden are almost done, & surprisingly good, I think.'[4] In a letter to Vita at the end of the month: 'We've made another pond too. At first the water slanted up one way and down another. And now where can I buy pots, Italian, and a statue? That's my contribution to the garden.'[5] There is no recorded reply from Vita and the provenance of the chosen pots and statues sadly are not Italian but rather the grocer's shop in Barcombe. Moreover it is hard to forgive Leonard, when by his own admission funds were not tight, for rejecting York stone in favour of the cheaper (by a few pounds only) concrete paving slabs. Was it about this area that Vita was

thinking when she responded thus to Virginia's request for an opinion about the garden, 'You cannot recreate Versailles on a quarter-acre of Sussex. It just cannot be done.'[6] Virginia also mentions an expedition to buy yew trees in September 1933 – perhaps this became the line of yew trees to the very west of this strip of land, in front of which the two shepherdesses now stand. Is it fanciful to suggest that in Tuscany they visited gardens filled with statuary and swagged pots of lemon trees, and made plans, over picnics in olive groves, to create an Italian-style garden at Monk's House? Or perhaps, wishfully, Leonard was thinking of the Italian statues around the rectangular pond at Garsington.

By the gate is a large lime tree which was planted before 1919. I was amused to find that Virginia shared my concern that this tree would blow down in a storm and land on the house. It was up this lime tree that Mitzi, Leonard's pet marmoset, escaped one day and refused to come down, not tempted even by the bait of honey, her favourite treat. Leonard had taken Mitzi in on a temporary basis to nurse her back to health. They took to each other and Mitzi stayed, inseparable from Leonard and intensely jealous. With a perfect understanding of his pet's nature, he summoned Virginia to the bottom of the lime tree and proceeded to kiss her. Instantly Mitzi leapt down from the tree in a jealous rage. Every time I weeded or planted white narcissi and hyacinths under that tree I thought of them standing beneath it, kissing, with a marmoset flying through the branches to oust the competition.

By September 1933, Virginia was able to write: 'I had so much of the most profound interest to write here – a dialogue of the soul with the soul, - & I have let it slip – why? Because of feeding the gold fish, of looking at the new pond, of playing bowls . . . Happiness.'[7]

ABOVE The Italian Garden in winter.
RIGHT Jim Bartholomew's plan of 1932 on page 191 shows that the enormous yew tree was once Leonard's topiary oeuvre: 'Did I tell you we are gradually carving a recumbent peacock – year by year – now his tail, now his neck?'[8] It is entirely possible that, the site having been that of a parsonage, the yew was already in situ in 1919 and that Leonard merely shaped it.
OPPOSITE *Rosa* 'Félicité Perpétue' on the south-facing but shady wall of the house.

A narrow bed in dry shade

Dry shade. Dreadful words. The chalky soil, flint walls and numerous trees at Monk's House forced us to experiment with different planting for dry shade over the years. This bed is inspired by the long narrow bed flanking the front path by the gate. It is shady – although some light filters through the trees above – and bone dry. These are the plants we used at varying times over the years.

Opposite this bed, in a tiny planting hole on a south-facing but incredibly shady wall, my favourite workhorse of a rose, 'Félicité Perpétue', flourishes. Under the elm tree by the gate we planted white epimediums, thalia, narcissi, wood anemones and some tiny wild strawberries. Sweet woodruff also does well scrambling around the gaps. For spring, thread some white narcissi and 'L'Innocence' hyacinths through the bed, and have some short white Cosmos 'Sonata' ready to fill gaps later in the summer.

1 *Anemone* x *hybrida* 'Honorine Jobert'
2 *Liriope muscari* – slow to establish but so useful, flourishing in the darkest spaces.
3 *Vibernum tinus* 'Eve Price', clipped into a ball.
4 *Cosmos bipinnatus* Sonata series. We used to plant these out where Thalia narcissi had flowered, leaving the hazel twig supports in place for the cosmos to grow through.
5 *Omphalodes* resembles a white forget-me-not but is more delicate, with larger, round leaves.
6 *Gillenia trifoliata*
7 *Euphorbia hypericifolia* 'Diamond Frost' continues the job of *Omphalodes* through the summer. It is tender and has to be brought into a greenhouse over winter.
8 *Geranium macrorrhizum* 'Album'. Another geranium that works well in dry shade is *G. phaeum* 'Mourning Widow', although it is taller and not as tidy in habit.

OPPOSITE CLOCKWISE FROM TOP LEFT The starry white flowers of *Gillenia trifoliata*, one of my favourite perennials. *Anemone* x *hybrida* 'Honorine Jobert' (Japanese anemones). The intriguing *Liriope muscari*, happy in dry shade.

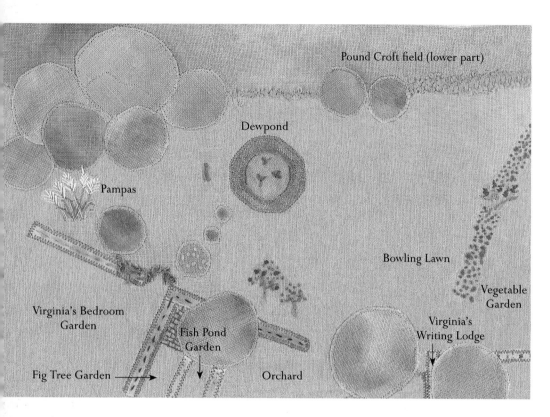

Pound Croft field (lower part)

Dewpond

Pampas

Bowling Lawn

Vegetable Garden

Virginia's Bedroom Garden

Fish Pond Garden

Virginia's Writing Lodge

Fig Tree Garden →

Orchard

The Terrace

Almost as soon as the Woolfs moved into Monk's House they recognised that acquiring the upper part of Pound Croft field would not only allow them to extend the garden but also protect the view and their privacy. Yet Virginia admitted in her diary in September 1926 that she and Leonard had quarrelled about 'his assumption that we can afford to saddle ourselves with a whole time gardener, build or buy him a cottage, & take in the terrace to be garden. Then, I said, we shall be tying ourselves to come here; shall never travel; & it will be assumed that Monk's House is the hub of the world. This it certainly is not, I said, to me; nor do I wish to spend such a measure of our money on gardens when we cannot buy rugs, beds or good arm chairs.'[1]

RIGHT In 1936 Vita gave the Woolfs three Lombardy poplars which were planted in a line across the Terrace. These were recalled by Lady Spender when she visited the garden with the National Trust, many years later. A third poplar should be added when the laburnum dies.

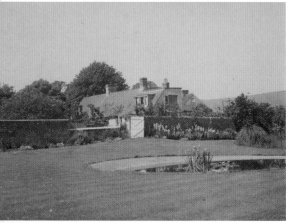

TOP Leonard and Virginia with Pinka.
ABOVE A long flower border ran the length of the flint wall dividing the Terrace from the rest of the garden. When Virginia writes from the top floor of the extension in 1931, 'I have come up here on this last evening to clear up papers. All is softly grey: L.'s yellow dahlias are burning on the edge of the terrace ...'[6] it is this border she is writing about. The Woolfs liked this view of the Terrace so much they had this postcard printed. One was sent to George Bernard Shaw in 1940. Note the large wooden gate and the gap in the wall where the old writing lodge used to be.
OPPOSITE The pampas grass was planted by Leonard. There had been pampas at Talland House, Virginia's childhood holiday home in Cornwall.

One suspects that Monk's House had indeed become the hub of Leonard's world, and while Virginia had always known he would fall in love with the garden, at the same time she occasionally resented the 'tremendous draw' it exerted upon him. Mostly, Virginia revelled in Leonard's transformation of the garden and enjoyed the pleasure it gave him. At other times she sensed the garden taking Leonard away from her. In the early years at the house she insisted they planned time for walks together. When Virginia was cross with Leonard she would complain 'we are watering the earth with our money'.[2] When she felt fondly towards him she would buy him a fish basin or statue. Yet only days before their argument about buying the field, Virginia had written in her diary 'God knows I wish we could buy the terrace, & have a garden all round the lodge. . .'[3] This was in 1926 and by 1928 there was enough money coming in for both garden and good chairs, and the field was an addition that would bring the Woolfs great pleasure.

The 'whole-time gardener' was Percy Bartholomew, who had moved to Rodmell after the war with his wife Lydia, and had been working for Leonard part-time since 1926. After acquiring the field Leonard needed full-time help in the garden and Percy was hired in November 1928, for a salary of £2 a week and free accommodation at Number 1 Park Cottages. Percy and Leonard worked together in the garden for nearly twenty years, arguing often, each resigning from and dismissing the other at least once, though never going through with it. 'Percy gave notice yesterday. Something about leaving lilies in the shed did the trick. You don't like what I do- &c . . . Whether final or not God knows . . . These things always blow up once every other year.'[4] Clearly though, the garden was a force for bonding as much as a source of arguments, for they also gossiped as they gardened – 'on and on they go – like old gaffers in gaiters'.[5] When in September 1938 it was announced on the BBC that Hitler had invited Chamberlain to Munich, Leonard rushed immediately into the garden to tell Percy.

Almost immediately after acquiring the field Percy and Leonard started to move the kitchen garden to the north-east corner of the Terrace. Five yews were planted along the edge of the Terrace and a hawthorn hedge around the vegetable beds and fruit cage, shown on the plan of the garden drawn in 1932 by Percy's older son Jim (see page 191). In August 1932, Leonard staked out a large saucer-shaped pond on the edge of the Terrace, inspired by the shallow dew ponds to be found up on the Sussex Downs. He chose a spot where the pond would reflect the branches of 'Leonard' and 'Virginia'.

The year had started sadly for the Woolfs, with the death in January of Lytton Strachey from cancer, followed weeks later by Dora Carrington's suicide. Lytton's death affected them deeply, and Virginia's letters to Carrington show her to have been an extremely kind and practical friend; indeed they visited Carrington at Ham Spray the day before she shot herself. Years before, Lytton had proposed to Virginia realising even as he uttered the words that it 'would be death' if she accepted. She did not, and so it was Lytton who encouraged Leonard to return from Ceylon to woo Virginia for himself: 'She's the only woman

LEFT The statue of David and Goliath was sculpted by Norman Mommens, who lived at South Heighton with his wife, the artist and potter Ursula in the 1950s. Three jugs made by Ursula are in the house today and she was delighted to see them there when she came for afternoon tea with us, in her early nineties, wearing bright red lipstick and complaining bitterly about the recent withdrawal of her driving licence.

OPPOSITE This view of the laburnum is a pleasure afforded only to those who live at Monk's House, as the light falls through it in this magical way after closing time.

ABOVE A painting of the view from
the Terrace by Vanessa Bell. This is the
view of the water meadows to Mount
Caburn with 'our hot pokers burning
on the steep'.[11] Researching this book
I discovered this painting was for sale
and the National Trust purchased it
for the house.
ABOVE RIGHT Leonard feeding the
fish in the dew pond.
OPPOSITE The view of the Terrace
looking back towards the house.
Compare this to the view in the
postcard to George Bernard Shaw
on page 110. The magnolia has grown
into the gap in the wall, and the long
border was turfed over in 1980.
Now that the Trust are in residence,
rather than a tenant, they could
consider re-instating the long border.

in the world with sufficient brains; its [sic] a miracle she should exist.'[7] Years later
Virginia reflected 'had I married Lytton I should never have written anything . . .
L. may be severe; but he stimulates. Anything is possible with him.'[8] Nonetheless,
she minded Lytton's death to the end of her days. Lytton was one of the frequent
visitors to Monk's House in the 1920s although he bemoaned the lack of
creature comforts to their friends – Virginia's photograph albums are full of
pictures of him in the garden, elegantly cross-legged in a comfortable cane chair.

The expanse of lawn between the kitchen garden and the dew pond was
where the Woolfs played bowls, with each other and with friends. Leonard was
surprisingly sporty – he played tennis with the rector's daughter, played the odd
game of cricket (in later years remembering the 'satisfaction of hitting a six over
long-on's head'[9]) and was very competitive at bowls. He met his match in Virginia
and hardly a summer evening went by without a game. 'Now I am going to beat L.
at bowls, on a fine blowing evening with the children playing with their dolls in
the meadow, all the trees in blossom, and some heat in the sun for a wonder.'[10]

Apart from the five stately yew trees, the edge of the Terrace was kept clear.
The view was precious to Virginia and she raged over the erection of sheds and
farm buildings which spoiled it. I am glad she did not suffer the sight of County
Hall, Lewes. When the Trust acquired the house, they recognized the importance
of the view, but were also mindful of unsightly changes beyond the boundary.
They planted two lime trees and an assortment of shrubs and smaller trees. A
year before we left, the Virginia Woolf Society pointed out to the Trust that the
view was becoming obscured. Letters passed back and forth but no decisions were
taken. On a Sunday in our last autumn, the South Downs Volunteers arrived, keen
to tackle a project. So we gave the order to attack and they cleared a considerable
amount. The Trust have continued this work and the view to Caburn is clear
again. Two of the five yews remain and it would be nice to replace the other three.

The Writing Lodge

Although some money had been spent on improving conditions in the converted toolshed, Virginia decided, having acquired the Terrace, to move her writing lodge to its current position, tucked in the corner of the Orchard from where she could enjoy the view over the water meadows. 'We are discussing plans for moving this lodge to the churchyard wall under the tree. Wicks' estimate is for £157 – which seems extreme. Considering that its only a fad: will improve the view but then perhaps an improved view is worth £157.'[1]

ABOVE AND RIGHT The writing lodge. In Virginia's lifetime it was half the size it is now; the part to the right of the tree was added after she died and now contains an exhibition about the house.

'It is not an ordinary desk, not such a desk as you might buy in London or Edinburgh you see in anybodies [sic] house when you go to lunch; this desk is a sympathetic one, full of character, trusty, discreet, very reserved.' Virginia Woolf

'My Lodge is demolished; the new house in process of building in the orchard. There will be open doors in front; & a view right over to Caburn. I think I shall sleep there on summer nights.'[2] By December the new lodge, with a new apple loft above, was finished. A small brick terrace was added in 1935 for £11, and this became the favourite place to gather with friends in deckchairs to talk, take tea and watch games of bowls. The delivery which saved the old woman from further debate with Virginia about the existence of God was a large crate containing a 'vast writing desk' she had bought for £6 10s. 'It is not an ordinary desk, not such a desk as you might buy in London or Edinburgh you see in anybodies [sic] house when you go to lunch; this desk is a sympathetic one, full of character, trusty, discreet, very reserved.'[3]

The writing room is almost certainly tidier than when Virginia was in occupation. Leonard described her as an 'untidy liver . . . Her room tended to become not merely untidy but squalid.'[4] She wrote the very first drafts of her novels in long hand, sitting in a low armchair. Later in the day she would sit at the desk to type up what she had written and further revisions were always typed. Revisions were also carried out in the bath, or on the long walks she took in the afternoons.

According to Leonard Virginia was, when well, very disciplined about working, making the journey across the garden to her writing lodge 'with the daily regularity of a stockbroker'.[5] Virginia puts it rather more poetically '[Tomorrow I] shall smell a red rose; shall gently surge across the lawn (I move as if I carried a basket of eggs on my head) light a cigarette, take my writing board on my knee; and let myself down, like a diver, very cautiously into the last sentence I wrote yesterday.'[6]

ABOVE Virginia's desk. The card folders bear labels with her writing, working folders for her novels.
ABOVE RIGHT Outside the writing lodge, left to right: Angelica Bell, Vanessa Bell, Clive Bell, Virginia Woolf, Maynard Keynes and Lydia Lopokova (legs only).

ABOVE The garden at sunrise.
The effect of this view on the
senses, 'The buzz, the croon,
the smell, all seemed to press
voluptuously against some
membrane; not to burst it; but to
hum round one such a complete
rapture of pleasure that I stopped,
smelt; looked. But again I cannot
describe that rapture.'[11]
OPPOSITE *Cosmos bipinnatus*
'Purity' in the Walled Garden,
grown from seed each year.

In 1936 Virginia suffered a prolonged bout of illness. The strain of working on *The Years* had overwhelmed her and she 'stuffed the proofs . . . away in a cupboard' and spent nearly three months at Monk's House leading a 'peaceful, lonely life which becomes extremely soothing. I work most of the morning; so does Leonard; and we walk and play bowls and cook dinner.'[7] Virginia complained that she was 'always losing [Leonard] in the garden'[8] and yet the garden was a source of comfort and delight to her, lying in the sun, looking at the apples and pokers, picking raspberries or strawberries for supper, bottling gooseberries, making jam. 'It's lovely in the garden; Leonard's flowers suddenly light up in the evening.'[9] Stuffed in a cupboard or not, *The Years* were fermenting and caused her more torment than any other novel; 'never another long book for me'[10] she wrote in her diary.

It is worth taking a moment to remember that Leonard and Virginia were fantastically hard-working, sharing a similar work ethic, each respecting the other's need to work and to have private space in which to do so. From the early 1920s they were at the centre of London literary life, running a small but successful publishing house and writing articles and reviewing for several newspapers and periodicals. They attended and gave lectures and talks; Virginia was being 'taken up' by the BBC. In London they rarely dined alone, often attended social events or went to the theatre, opera or ballet. They travelled. They 'travelled' the Hogarth Press books, a quaint euphemism for sales trips. All the while Virginia was working on *The Years*, *Three Guineas* was simmering in the same pot, and papers to read for the Roger Fry biography were pouring in. They wrote letters and kept diaries, and Leonard kept meticulous records of everything, from the seeds he planted to the music they listened to on the gramophone. They were both politically active; Leonard was Secretary to the Executive Committees of the Labour Party for many years, and Virginia involved herself in feminist and anti-Fascist politics. They had, for their time and class, minimal domestic help.

ABOVE This needlepoint seat cover was worked on in part by Virginia.
RIGHT The blotter on Leonard's desk bears witness to his different interests and activities.

'*Back from a good week end at Rodmell – a week end of no talking, sinking at once into deep safe book reading; & then sleep: clear, transparent; with the may tree like a breaking wave outside; & all the garden green tunnels, mounds of green: & then to wake into the hot still day, & never a person to be seen, never an interruption: the place to ourselves: the long hours.*' Virginia Woolf

The Years was published on 15 March 1937. Virginia dreaded the reaction 'I'm going to be beaten, I'm going to be laughed at, I'm going to be held up to scorn and ridicule.'[12] In fact, it sold more copies than any of her previous novels and the critics were mostly kind. Diary entries in June 1937 show her feeling much stronger, looking back to the summer of depression in 1936 and realising that she was now in 'a deep blue quiet space . . . beyond harm.'[13] In the first months of 1937 her preoccupations were *Three Guineas*, Leonard's health (diabetes was suspected), the death of the manager at the Hogarth Press and, most of all, her nephew Julian Bell's determination to fight in the Spanish Civil War. Following the bombing of Guernica in April 1937, Leonard and Virginia took part in a fund-raising meeting at the Albert Hall in aid of the 4,000 Basque refugee children who had been evacuated to England. In July 1937 the news came that Julian had died of wounds received driving an ambulance in Spain. The Woolfs dropped everything, remaining at Monk's House until October, Virginia visiting Vanessa almost daily and writing in between, 'keeping life going when otherwise it would have stopped'[14] as Vanessa later confided to Vita Sackville-West, asking her to tell Virginia. It was in the shadow of this sad death that Virginia finished *Three Guineas*, a work of non-fiction providing a passionate and pacifist answer to the question of a fictional young barrister 'How are we to prevent war?', confessing to Vanessa that she was 'completely stuck on my war pamphlet . . . I'm always wanting to argue it with Julian – in fact I wrote it as an argument with him.'[15]

Leonard's health problems continued, although tests revealed nothing serious. His hand tremor, a lifelong affliction, worsened and he took up the Alexander technique in an attempt to improve it, with some success. Perhaps his symptoms were of stress caused by Virginia's 1936 illness, Julian's death and a better understanding than most that war was inevitable. He wrote later that for the two years before war broke out in 1939 he felt 'deeply and bitterly' that 'The world was reverting . . . to Barbarism.'[16] It was against this background that Leonard gardened in 1937, clipping the yews, battling the slugs on his zinnias and redesigning the Walled Garden.

LEFT Sweet pea 'Cupani' grown from seed each year for the Millstone Terrace border and *Allium* 'Gladiator' about to break out. OPPOSITE '& all the garden green tunnels, mounds of green.'[17]

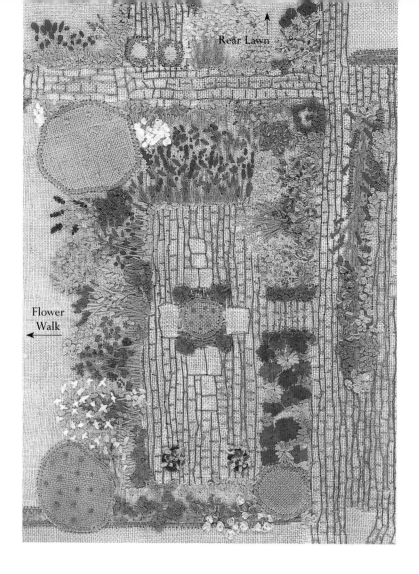

The Walled Garden

Gaining a greater understanding of how much the central part we call the Walled Garden has evolved since the Woolfs bought Monk's House has been one of the great pleasures of researching this book. In 1919 the smoothly rolled lawn extended all the way up to the flint wall that now borders the Orchard. On the 1920 conveyance of the parcel of land now forming the Italian Garden three outbuildings are shown in the middle of the garden, a laundry (large enough to have a chimney stack which blew off over the Christmas of 1921), the aforementioned earth closet 'discretely [sic], but ineffectively, hidden in a grove of cherry laurels'[1] and the remains of a granary.

RIGHT A 'blaze' of dahlias – Requiem, Gerrie Hoek and Ludwig Helfert.

An 'immense gaunt cherry tree grew out of a flower border into which the cabbages had somewhat penetrated'[1]. This is the cherry tree at the front of the archive picture on page 134. It is only by realising how the garden looked in 1919 that Leonard's gift for garden making can start to be appreciated.

In 1922 Leonard demolished the old laundry and the earth closet and created a small brick terrace in their place. Otherwise the area now filled by the Walled Garden was a large flower bed, with cordon and espalier-trained fruit trees, flowers and vegetables. Having laid the paths and Millstone Terrace in 1930 and created the Flower Walk in front of the yew hedge, in 1937 Leonard turned once again to the central part of the garden.

The fruit trees had begun to obscure the view of the Downs and were shading the plants beneath. At the end of August 1937 Mr Wicks, the builder in Rodmell, was summoned to discuss and plan 'Leonard's new folly, another pond and a bricked garden'.[2] The smaller fruit trees which had been planted in 1922 were removed, leaving only the two old cherry trees and one other fruit

OPPOSITE I always longed to replace the two cherry trees in this part of the garden but there were concerns about the paths. We inherited the weeping pear (left of picture) but it died two years before we left, and was replaced with an apple tree. In late summer the Walled Garden is layered with rich colours, crowned by the vivid orange trumpets of the Chinese trumpet vine, *Campsis grandiflora*, on the old granary wall.
ABOVE *Persicaria* 'Firetail' and orange crocosmia fight for supremacy below the campsis.

RIGHT *Allium* 'Gladiator'.
BELOW A photograph from the 1930s showing the Walled Garden in spring with a copy of Donatello's David standing beneath the cherry tree and the fish basins filled with water.

OPPOSITE The Walled Garden in June. The campsis foliage is a fresh green, echoing that of the euphorbia and providing a foil for the quieter June colours of the lavender Munstead, *Campanula poscharskyana* and *Nepeta* 'Six Hills Giant' in the swagged stone pots beyond.

tree, all growing within the flower beds surrounding the terrace made of bricks interspersed with large stone slabs.

The original plan was to sink another lily pond into the centre. Perhaps Leonard found the fish basins and fancied them instead, or perhaps the expense of the lily pond caused him to revise his plan. He wrote to Philcox Bros to let them know that 'the two basins which I have purchased will require some little repairing to make them water tight . . . they should also be raised 1½ feet from the ground when placed in position. Would it be possible to do something so that one could drain the water out of them in cold weather?'[3]

It was Virginia who purchased the basins, out of her 'hoard', from a shop in Handcross, driving down to Monk's House on a wet day in September 1937. On 22 October Virginia wrote ' . . . we're off . . . to our garden, via a Grocer's shop in Crawley, where Leonard is going to buy a leaden Cupid for his new water garden. He has a passion for ponds: and whenever the grocer has a cupid to sell, we buy it, to stand naked, with a tortoise balanced on the bow.'[4] Whether this fanciful flight of a cupid (betraying a teasingly indulgent attitude to Leonard's obsession with his garden) found its match in reality we do not know but a couple of days later she wrote: 'The new garden ready, save for the basins still to be embedded. The view is now clear through the walled garden to the down.'[5]

The Walled Garden faces south; even so, with two large cherry trees the planting must have been confined to bulbs and shade-tolerant plants. A stray crinum lily used to come up every year on the corner where one cherry tree stood. Looking at the photograph on page 134 it is clearly summer (there are zinnias in the bed surrounding the lawn) and yet the bed on the right of the entrance to the Walled Garden appears to be host to creeping thymes and alpines, an assortment of which are mentioned in Leonard's gardening notebooks. The photograph left was taken a few years later and shows that in the spring Leonard grew daffodils and spring bulbs in profusion around the cherry trees. John Lehmann remembered driving through Lewes with Leonard and spotting a terracotta copy of the Donatello David in the window of an antiques

'. . . we are safe in our garden, and it's the most I can do to get Leonard to leave it.' Virginia Woolf

PREVIOUS PAGES: LEFT Many of the dahlias in Leonard's notebooks are shades of pinks and purples.
RIGHT Allium 'Gladiator' and sweet rocket work well together in early summer.

RIGHT Taken by John Lehmann in 1938, this shows the Walled Garden completed. Note the box hedge flanking the path on the right; it is now a cavity wall.

OPPOSITE AND ABOVE Philadelphus is wonderful in June but a little dull thereafter. Clematis continues the theme, followed later by a honeysuckle with bright golden flowers.

shop. Leonard was very taken with it, so much so he bought it 'without haggling'. For years it stood under the cherry tree in the Walled Garden. Today there is no shade. The cherry trees died long ago. David lies in two pieces awaiting funds for repair and the fish basins no longer hold water.

With the completion of the Walled Garden in 1937 the garden was laid out more or less as it is today. In September 1937, the kitchen was painted a vivid green (I believe traces of the colour are visible on the edge of the Heal's dresser in the kitchen), and a new window installed next to the back door. Virginia pronounced the kitchen 'a great success – now green & cool, & the new window shows a square of flowers. Why, all these years, I never thought to lay out £20 on a new cupboard, paint & window, I don't know.'[6] This is the window on page 24, and the green is similar to that of the chair on the left in the same picture.

Monk's House was now 'luxurious to the point of having electric fires in the bedrooms'. At least the Woolfs felt it was, unless someone really grand threatened to visit, such as the decorator Sibyl Colefax, who was forewarned of the modest comforts in the following terms:

(1) view is ruined
(2) No room for chauffeur in house
(3) the smallest possible doghole for you
(4) village char is cook
with a ps 'No clothes but nightgowns worn here.'[7]

It seems that storage for clothes was an insoluble problem.

Writing to Vanessa at the end of the long summer spell at Monk's House in 1938, Virginia recalled saying to Leonard 'We get snatches of divine loneliness here . . . why not stay here for ever and ever, enjoying this immortal rhythm in which both soul and eye are at rest? So I said, and for once L said: You're not such a fool as you seem.'[8] Virginia wrote rapturously about the countryside and about Monk's House but was always torn between the country and London, between 'divine loneliness' and the 'hum and throb', whereas Leonard knew exactly where he liked best to be, and where it was probably best for Virginia to be, and that was in the garden at Monk's House.

'...crossing the garden by the pale flowers'

This border plan would be good for the end of a west-facing garden with a high boundary which could be draped in rose and clematis, as the backdrop to a cool planting scheme featuring some of Leonard Woolf's favourite flowers, including his 'vast white lilies' and an 'inflorescence of Japanese anemones'.

As with all planting schemes it can be expanded to work framed by large trees with a deeper border, in which case one might add a rose or two and another clematis on a support, but I have assumed the average narrow garden, with a fence at the end, perhaps with a gate. Underplant the trees and shrubs as much as possible with sweet woodruff, comfrey, white wood anemones and epimedium, with spring bulbs beneath.

Always try to plant new borders in the autumn so that you can underplant everything with bulbs. The lilies need their own space. I find it easier to plant them in large pond pots, nice and deep, and then lift them out after they have finished flowering. If you are really organised you could have some *Nicotiana sylvestris* in another pot ready to drop into the hole. Or more cosmos. 'Purity' grows well over a metre tall and fills awkward gaps with its feathery foliage and large white flowers.

OPPOSITE CLOCKWISE FROM TOP LEFT *Hydrangea arborescens* 'Annabelle', *Alchemilla mollis*, *Clematis montana*, *Astrantia major* var. *rosea*, *Cosmos bipinnatus* 'Purity' and the perfect creamy buds of *Rosa* 'Moonlight'.

1 *Anemone* x *hybrida* 'Honorine Jobert' (Japanese anemone)
2 *Euphorbia palustris*
3 *Geranium macrorrhizum* 'Bevan's Variety'
4 *Alchemilla mollis*
5 *Astrantia major* 'Alba' or, for a little more colour, *rosea*
6 *Echinacea purpurea* 'Alba'
7 *Gillenia trifoliata*
8 *Lilium regale*
9 *Hesperis matronalis* – purple (could have white) underplanted with *Allium* 'Gladiator'
10 *Tulipa* 'Triumphator' in spring followed by white cosmos 'Purity' (sown under glass and transplanted out)
11 *Lilium auratum* (Leonard's 'vast white lilies')
12 *Hydrangea arborescens* 'Annabelle'
13 *Syringa pubescens* ssp. *microphylla* 'Superba' – underplanted with hellebores, comfrey, Thalia narcissi and white wood anemone
14 *Amelanchier lamarckii* – underplanted with hellebores, *Epimedium grandiflorum* f. *violaceum* and Narcissi Thalia, as well as the hesperis and Japanese anemones
15 *Rosa* 'Moonlight'
16 *Magnolia stellata* – underplanted with snowdrops, wood anemones, for spring and sweet woodruff for summer
17 *Clematis montana* 'Alba'

Monk's House Dahlias

Dahlias feature in Virginia's descriptions of the garden from the start. Leonard always grew them, seemingly trying new varieties each year. Each year we ordered one or two new varieties from the Dahlia National Collection. We bought our first selection in 2001 from Sarah Raven because she is married to Vita's grandson Adam Nicolson, and we liked the connection.

'Leonard's garden has really been a miracle . . . such a blaze of dahlias that even today one feels lit up.'

Virginia Woolf

Part 4 The last page

In the summer of 1938 the garden was 'flowering in every colour'.[1]
The year had started worryingly, with Leonard suffering from kidney
problems and unable to make the usual pilgrimage to Rodmell to prune
the fruit trees. An outbreak of foot and mouth disease shut off the
countryside around Rodmell until late January, when they managed
a quick visit to Monk's House in torrential rain. Virginia was anxious
about the reception of *Three Guineas*, published in June, and had now
started to write the biography of Roger Fry. Leonard (privately) wished
she had not succumbed to the pressure to take on this project – it was
to cause Virginia considerable strain over the last years of her life. It is
the only work of hers about which he voiced his criticism.

OPPOSITE Vanessa Bell's 1912 portrait of Virginia, bought by the National Trust for the opening of Monk's House.
Below it are snowdrops and pulmonaria in a jug by Ursula Mommens. The fluted wooden column on the left is one
of a pair added by the Woolfs to either side of the dining room.

When they arrived for their summer break in August they found the workmen had started earlier than expected on the conversion of part of the attic into 'Hedgehog Hall', a long, extremely narrow library for Leonard. 'We've workmen dinging and donging: we are making our library, but it has suddenly given birth to a balcony and a verandah. I can't explain how.'[2] Tanks were engaging in manoeuvres up on the Downs; and aeroplanes were 'on the prowl'. England was preparing for war throughout 1938. 'L&I no longer talk about it. Much better to play bowls and pick dahlias. They're blazing in the sitting room, orange against the black last night. Our balcony is up.'[3]

In retrospect the relief expressed in Virginia's diary after the Munich Agreement in September 1938 makes painful reading.

A year later war was again almost upon them. In London they had been forced to leave Tavistock Square and found a new home at 37 Mecklenburgh Square, but it was not yet habitable, which meant that they spent most of the summer in Rodmell.

At Monk's House there was a 'forest of dahlias and zinnias'[4]. Mornings were spent struggling with the biography of Roger Fry, evenings brought games of bowls on the Terrace. A short motoring holiday in June through Brittany and Normandy was to be Virginia's last journey abroad.

'I like country life, even with bombs, much better than London without. The garden is just beginning to break into life with crocuses and iris reticulata under the apple trees. We too had a pretty stiff winter here, very cold and snow . . .'
Leonard Woolf

OPPOSITE Dahlias, calendula, tithonia, crocosmia and fennel ready to set against the green paintwork of the drawing room.

ABOVE This is the only photograph I have been able to find of the greenhouse in the Orchard. It was 6 metres (20 feet) long × 3 metres (10 feet) high. If you look very carefully you can just make out the distinctive curved roof of the cactus house alongside it. Virginia was never keen on Leonard's greenhouses, calling them his Kew Gardens.

ABOVE RIGHT Angelica Bell, Virginia Woolf, Mary Hutchinson and Clive Bell bowling on the terrace.

In July 1939 war of a different kind broke out: the Affair of the Greenhouse. Leonard was rather keen on his greenhouses and already had a large one on the north-west wall of the Orchard: you can just see it in the corner of the picture of the Walled Garden above left. That month, he had started, without reference to Virginia, to build another with a base of pinkish bricks. As the new greenhouse went up, she became more unhappy: 'headache; guilt; remorse' she wrote in her diary. Conflict with Leonard was rare, and yet 'the ugliness: v: L's wish. And is it worth the misery? – oughtn't I to have said go ahead when he came to me in the bath this morning?' She didn't, and the greenhouse was pulled down. Relations were strained. Virginia wrote that morning ' . . . (I'm whistling to keep up my spirits this very strained grey day – the Greenhouse morning.) I must now carry off lunch. What annoys me is L.'s adroitness in fathering the guilt on me. His highhandedness. I see the temptation. "Oh you don't want it – so submit."' This made for a rather bad-tempered game of bowls that evening. Later in the evening Virginia asked of Leonard 'Do you ever think me beautiful now?' He replied 'The most beautiful of women.'[5] By the next day the 'great affair of the GH' had been settled. A cold house was to be built behind the existing greenhouse.

By August, war was imminent. 'Next week we go down to Sussex . . . will one be able to work? Will one have to fill the house with refugees? There are aeroplanes always round us; and air raid shelters – but I still believe we shall have peace.'[6] The Woolfs were at Monk's House when war was declared on Sunday 3 September. They helped with settling evacuees from London, most of whom found village life intolerable and went home within a few weeks.

Friends continued to visit when trains allowed and members of the Hogarth Press also came down to Rodmell for meetings. The winter of 1939–40 was bitter: 'Never was there such a medieval winter. The electricity broke down. We cooked over the fire, remained unwashed, slept in stockings and mufflers.'[7] Percy Bartholomew had to dig out paths and even the ink froze in Virginia's inkwell. Rationing was in force. Her diary reveals Virginia alternating between a sense that 'all creative power is lost' and tossing a myriad of different ideas around her brain, mostly set off by the war and the effect on the society around her, distracting her from the Roger Fry biography. After a bout of 'flu in the spring of 1940 she strolled on the Terrace and noticed 'gold thick clumps of crocuses' and, later, daffodils in 'luminous groups'.[8] Leonard was making the rock garden on the back of the granary wall and Percy was spraying the apples.

Finally, in May 1940, she posted the proofs of Roger Fry and felt some relief in doing so. As Holland and Belgium fell 'Apple blossom [was] snowing the garden' and a bowl had rolled into the dew pond. Suddenly Rodmell, just four miles from the English Channel, became more dangerous than London as invasion seemed inevitable in the weeks after Dunkirk. Leonard and Virginia had a 'rather matter of fact talk' about suicide in that event, for which Leonard had made provision with a supply of petrol with which to gas themselves with carbon monoxide in the garage, backed up by a supply of cyanide provided by Virginia's brother, Adrian. Then a most painful cry in Virginia's diary 'No, I don't want the garage to see the end of me. I've a wish for 10 years more, & to write my book wh.[ich] as usual darts into my brain.'[9]

In the garden the gooseberries suffered blight. Percy continued to dig the vegetable beds and mow the lawns. Eggs were pickled in jars and eaten for breakfast pretending not to notice the different taste. Virginia picked blackberries for jam. Leonard chaired the Vegetable Committee and in 1940 persuaded his tenant, Farmer Jansen, to lend their field back to the village for the growing of vegetables. Unsurprisingly, the Woolfs were not short of fruit and vegetables, and surpluses were given away to friends, bartered or sold. Vegetables from the field were also sold or exchanged. The Boys' School in Newhaven

'*Never was there such a medieval winter.
The electricity broke down. We cooked
over the fire, remained unwashed, slept
in stockings and mufflers.*' Virginia Woolf

LEFT The dew pond in winter.
BELOW Leonard skating on the pond in 1941. Only weeks later he would bury Virginia's ashes below the elm tree behind him.
OPPOSITE The Terrace in winter. Note that since this photograph was taken all of the growth along the boundary has been cleared.

'*The snow came down on Saturday, thick white cake sugar all over the garden . . .*'
Virginia Woolf

bought potatoes from Leonard at 7 shillings per cwt and asked if there was 'any farmer who is able to have carrots'. In 1940 Leonard applied for a permit to obtain 40 pounds of sugar for the bees. As he was producing honey it was a legitimate use of sugar at a time when it was tightly rationed (a week's ration was 8 oz). However, an independent person had to verify the number of hives he owned and where he intended to buy the sugar. By September the hives 'dripped pure gold'[10] and Virginia filled thirty bottles of honey. That month, the orchard yielded a record crop of plums: ' . . . you ought to come and see our garden, which is the apple of Leonard's eye. As you can imagine, I never do a hand's turn, but walk in the shade of the trees, and cant[sic] remember names.'[11]

Leonard also wrote to the Local Agricultural Committee about his greenhouses. He was entitled to heat his greenhouse for the production of produce, but being Leonard and straight as a die, he was worried that the return pipe in the second greenhouse was providing heat where he grew only flowers. This probably explains why, even in the freezing December of 1940, the greenhouse was full of carnations. The Committee was kind – the incidental heat from the hot return pipe was not regarded as a crime.

In August 1940 the War Office had imposed the construction of a pillbox in the Croft field and the war in the skies above Rodmell began in earnest. Virginia's letters continue to be energetic, amusing even, writing of 'Armada weather' as they played bowls beneath the planes flying overhead, shockingly low, on one occasion forcing them to fling themselves face down into the grass of the Orchard. She continued to take long walks, taking cover in haystacks if planes flew overhead. Leonard joined the village fire-fighting squad and Virginia, the Women's Institute, giving a couple of talks and arranging for others, including Vita Sackville-West and Angelica Bell, to do the same. The Woolfs were pulled into village life rather more than they were used to, and they did their bit uncomplainingly but it meant 'incessant human voices' interrupting and endless distractions. Monk's House was no longer a peaceful retreat. Yet Virginia continued to write *Between the Acts* (originally titled *Pointz Hall*) inspired by Rodmell life, almost as a relief from the 'drudgery' of Roger Fry.

In London, having just settled the Hogarth Press and their belongings into 37 Mecklenburgh Square, an air raid destroyed the house opposite and left an unexploded bomb in the garden of number 37. On being detonated, their new home was rendered uninhabitable. All the printing machinery, including the original hand press and type, was moved to Rodmell, together with all of their books. When Farmer Botten agreed to let them have three rooms for storage he had not envisaged a room full of inflammable books and papers. He withdrew his offer of one of the rooms, which meant that all of the books had to be stored elsewhere, including Monk's House, where they were piled up in great stacks on the damp brick floors of the big sitting room. The offices of the Press moved out to Letchworth, necessitating many tedious and convoluted wartime journeys for Leonard. All the possessions had to be unpacked, cleaned and stored. It took

BELOW Leonard had to seek authorisation for the purchase of enough sugar to feed his bees during the war. Today, as then, Monk's House garden is a paradise for every bug, bee and butterfly.

ABOVE Sugar rations were supplemented by the production of honey throughout the war.

four days, leaving Virginia exhausted, and yet full of grit, determined to 'scrub & polish & discard: & make our life here as taut & bright & vigorous as it can be'. For the first time in her life without a home in London, life really was 'restricted by the radius of the village'.[12] In her diaries Monk's House is referred to often as a 'little boat' or a 'ship' and although people came aboard for visits, they were not the people Virginia wanted to see.

Writing her diary one evening she looked out of the window to see ' the apples are red in the trees. L. is gathering them . . . And all the air a solemn stillness holds. Till 8.30 when the cadaverous twanging in the sky begins; the planes going to London . . . The elm tree sprinkling its little leaves against the sky. Our pear tree swagged with pears; . . . Should I think of death? Last night a great heavy plunge of bomb under the window. So near we both started. We went onto the terrace . . . All quiet . . . I said to L: I don't want to die yet.'[13] They were heading into another winter, 'a rather hard lap'.[14] Her friend and doctor, Octavia Wilberforce, was shocked to see how thin Virginia had become and started to send weekly deliveries of milk, cream and butter from Brighton; Virginia offering apples in exchange. Typically, Virginia could not resist flaunting these gifts to Ethel as 'my lover's cream'. Vita also sent presents of butter and the wool from her flock of Jacob sheep with which Louie knitted a thick warm jersey for Virginia: 'Its saved my life I live in it'.[15] Food became an obsession: 'How one enjoys food now: I make up imaginary meals,'[16] she wrote as 1940 ended.

The second winter of the war was as bitter as the first. Leonard skated on the lily pond. His skates still hang at Monk's House. In January, Virginia visited London and picked her way around the Bloomsbury squares, now 'gashed; dismantled; the old red bricks all white powder'.[17] Back at Monk's House she took to scrubbing floors and cleaning out the kitchen in an attempt to 'rout'

ABOVE Snowdrops in the garden. OPPOSITE The bust of Virginia by Stephen Tomlin. In this shady spot we often found small floral tributes, poetry, and once a pebble, inscribed with the words 'thank you for my room'.

depression. In the garden there were snowdrops. Virginia's diary entries are painfully flat, yet her letters show a brave face. 'This trough of despair shall not, I swear, engulf me.' Yet they seemed to be living 'without a future . . . [their] noses pressed to a closed door'.[18] By March it was evident that Virginia was seriously ill. Leonard was beside himself. Octavia Wilberforce had been visiting once a week on the pretext of bringing the milk and cream, but in reality to check up on Virginia at Leonard's request. On the morning of 28 March he wrote to John Lehmann to say that Virginia was 'on the verge of a complete nervous breakdown and is seriously ill. The war, food&cold have been telling on her and I have seen it coming on for some time.'[19]

On 28 March Virginia helped Louie with some dusting, wrote letters of unbearable sadness to Vanessa and Leonard, walked to the River Ouse, filled her pockets with stones and jumped in. She would have had to jump. The banks of the Ouse are high and steep and the tidal river fast-flowing. Her last diary entry concerned the garden: 'L is doing the rhododendrons.'[20]

Virginia's body was found several weeks later by children playing near Southease Bridge. Leonard had to identify her body, driven to the mortuary by the same policeman who only weeks before had delivered a severe reprimand to Virginia about a chink of light in their blackout, which had upset her greatly. She was cremated at the Downs Crematorium in Brighton, with only Leonard present. Later he buried her ashes under one of the elms in the garden, placing a stone tablet at the spot engraved with the last words of *The Waves*. This tablet was found on the bank years later and placed under the Stephen Tomlin bust.

Despite all the comfort and support from Vanessa, Vita and Octavia Wilberforce, Leonard blamed himself for not taking drastic action the moment he saw Virginia was on the verge of another breakdown. Mindful that Virginia's 1913 suicide attempt was made the day after seeing a specialist, Leonard felt it had been risky taking Virginia to see Octavia Wilberforce on 27 March. Some time after her death Leonard read her diary. The last few entries are full of disturbing images, almost like being in a hall of distorting mirrors. Virginia had once described Leonard as having the look of a man upon the gallows when she did not behave in ways prescribed by him to keep her well. In those last weeks did she notice the old symptoms returning, her suspicions confirmed by that look and the last visit to Octavia? Leonard would not allow himself to be comforted. He did not want company. He wrote:

They say "Come to tea and let us comfort you". But it's no good. One must be crucified on one's own private cross . . . I know that V. will not come across the garden from the lodge, & yet I look in that direction for her. I know that she is drowned & yet I listen for her to come on at the door. I know that it is the last page & yet I turn it over.[21]

'Against you I will fling myself unvanquished and unyielding, O Death.

The waves broke on the shore.'

The Waves

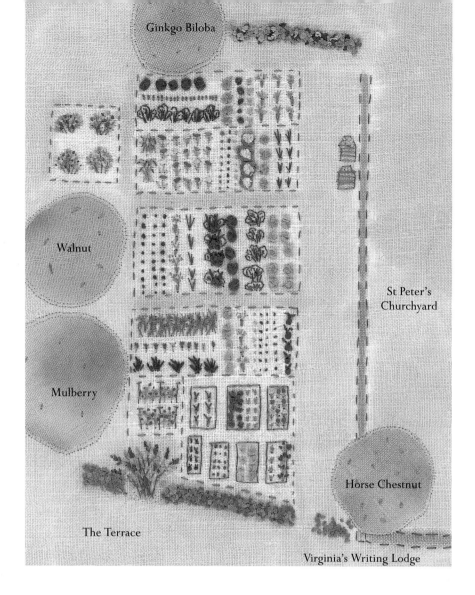

Ginkgo Biloba

Walnut

Mulberry

The Terrace

St Peter's
Churchyard

Horse Chestnut

Virginia's Writing Lodge

The Vegetable Garden

Jacob Verrall tended a magnificent vegetable garden at Monk's
House. He was helped by his gardener, William Dedman,
who was also the sexton of St Peter's Church Rodmell. When
Leonard bought Monk's House, William wrote to ask whether
he would like help with planting out vegetables for 'it is quite
time they was in if they are to be ready in the winter and the
spring'. William helped Leonard in the garden until the garden
was extended in 1928. In the papers at Sussex University there
are carbon copies of vegetable planting plans for each year,
noting when and how vegetables were sown. After 1928, Percy
Bartholomew ran the Vegetable Garden, although arguments
between Percy and Leonard were frequent.

RIGHT Flowers and vegetables fill the the neat plots.

THIS PAGE Today the Vegetable Garden is divided into allotments managed by the village horticultural association. We installed raised beds for the area reserved for Monk's House tenants. The method of supporting sweet peas and beans (left) is copied from the kitchen garden at Charleston.

As Percy's daughter Marie told me: 'Dad liked to do everything by the book.' She remembers her father sitting down to dinner each night grumbling that 'Woolf has been spuddling around again.' The task of moving the Vegetable Garden to the north-east corner of the Terrace would have been considerable. Two hawthorn hedges were laid at right angles to protect the Vegetable Garden on the north and western sides. A large fruit cage dominated the middle portion of the garden, with gooseberries, every colour of currant, strawberries and raspberries. The soil was improved. There is testy correspondence between Leonard and his tenant farmer, relating to a lorry-load of manure getting stuck in November mud at the entrance to the field. When the cesspool filled up Percy had the delightful job of emptying it onto the vegetable beds with a bucket.

When the Woolfs were in London, Percy sent a hamper by train each week. Leonard treated the growing of fruit and vegetables like a business; surplus was sold at the local Women's Institute market and the profits recorded each year. Fruit was bottled. Virginia's niece Angelica remembered 'the pride she took in her cupboard of jade-green gooseberries and sad-purple raspberries on the stairs at Monk's House'.[1] Surprisingly, at her first encounter with Elizabeth Bowen Virginia mused on the idea of making gooseberry ice cream . . . would the colour be that of the fruit, she wondered.

At some point the hawthorn hedge shown on the northern edge of the kitchen garden in Jim Bartholomew's plan of 1932 (see page 191) was removed, possibly at the same time that a mulberry and walnut tree were planted. These trees have recently been dated and are at least seventy years old. I think it likely they were planted by Leonard in the early days of his relationship with Trekkie since I doubt Virginia would have countenanced the planting of such large trees in the way of her view. Leonard co-founded the Rodmell Horticultural Society in 1941, chairing its meetings in the green drawing room at Monk's House. The most coveted trophy in the Rodmell summer show is the Leonard Woolf Rose Bowl for the best exhibit, presented by Trekkie in 1970 in memory of Leonard. In the summer of 1968, the last summer show of his life, Leonard (with the help of his new gardener Vout van der Keift) won six first prizes for vegetables. Percy had developed problems with his eyes and resigned in 1946. Today the kitchen garden has been turned over to allotments for the village. One is kept by Ron Medhurst, the shepherd from South Farm, now over 90, and his wife, Dot, who served in the land army during the war. Their allotment is how I imagine Leonard's kitchen garden to have been: everything done by the book, serried ranks of immaculate vegetables, clearly labelled, with never a weed in sight.

'In his beautiful garden time is suspended.' Prof Asa Briggs

Part 5 After Virginia

After Virginia's death Monk's House was the hub of Leonard's life.
He took rooms in London, but they were a convenient base rather
than a home. His routine continued much as before. In the mornings
he worked at the little desk high up in Hedgehog Hall, his chair
in front of the French windows, facing the fireplace with its Cozy
stove where years before Morgan Forster had burned his trousers
trying to get dry after a walk. In the afternoon he gardened and the
evenings were spent reading and listening to music, although now
the garden was sometimes a lure after supper as well.

ABOVE Leonard with Coco outside the front door (never used) at Monk's House.
OPPOSITE The border flanking the lawn from the lawn, a tangle of *Salvia* x *sylvestris* 'Mainacht', lysimachia,
verbascums and lavender.

LEFT Two jugs by Ursula Mommens
on the bookcase in Virginia's
bedroom, where translated editions
of her novels are kept.
OPPOSITE ABOVE Trekkie
in the cactus house.
OPPOSITE BELOW Trekkie and
Leonard beekeeping in the Orchard.
BELOW Tucked into the blotter
on Leonard's desk the compliments
slip for the Hogarth Press and some
1930s seed packets which we found
and gave to the house.

Troops were often billeted in the adjacent field. Leonard gave them apples and vegetables and played chess with the officers, who occasionally stayed in the rooms over the garage where he also kept boxes of Virginia's works in translation. One day he found a Czech officer reading in the garden, ecstatic at having found a book in his native language. It was *Flush*.

In August 1941, Leonard joined the board of the *New Statesman* and after trying spare rooms in various friends' homes took a set of rooms in Cliffords Inn, where he and Virginia had started married life some twenty-two years earlier. He stayed in London for two or three nights a week, later moving back to a couple of rooms in 37 Mecklenburgh Square. He started to visit old friends again, including Tom Eliot, to whom he took a box of dahlias from the garden.

Another renewed friendship was with Alice Ritchie, a writer who had also worked as a sales representative for the Hogarth Press in the early 1930s, and whose two novels had been published by the press. Alice had introduced Leonard to her younger sister Trekkie, an art student at the Slade and, as Leonard later recalled, 'extremely beautiful'. The sisters had been brought up in South Africa but the family returned to England when their father served in the Great War. The Hogarth Press commissioned Trekkie to design the covers for Alice's novels and a few more titles. Now Alice was dying of cancer and was staying with Trekkie and her husband, Ian Parsons, a director at Chatto & Windus, at a house in Victoria Square. Here she invited Leonard to visit her. He continued to do so each week until she died in October 1941. Trekkie was grateful to him; she had to work at the War Office and was comforted to know Alice had company.

At the beginning of 1942 Leonard left a box of white freesias and a red cyclamen on Trekkie's doorstep. Immediately she wrote to thank him, lamenting the lack of a place in which to garden, telling him how much she had always coveted a greenhouse. There followed several doorstep offerings: strawberries, apples, pears, more freesias interspersed with letters exchanging news about pets and plants. Trekkie's first letters are charming, ever so slightly flirtatious, and entirely undemanding. She sent him seeds for 'delicious little marrows'. By February 1943 Leonard has become 'so very good at working [her] out' and is bringing her his precious *Iris reticulata* to paint. By the summer, Leonard had taken a lease on the neighbouring house in Victoria Square and Trekkie was spending weekends at Monk's House.

Leonard was in love and did not refrain from declaring himself. Trekkie was happily married to Ian Parsons, even though they were not sleeping together and he was having an affair with Norah Smallwood, a partner at Chatto. Trekkie warned Leonard that while she welcomed his love and indeed returned it, she did not want it to cause either of them unhappiness. This caveat issued, they embarked on a deeply romantic, if technically chaste, love affair and one thing they shared with intense delight was the garden at Monk's House. Trekkie was a very keen gardener and they enjoyed working together in the garden at Monk's House.

Leonard's time in Ceylon and Trekkie's in South Africa had left both with a liking for exotic, brightly coloured flowers. They collaborated on an article about the stapelia, or African starfish plant, carnivorous and stinking repellently of dead meat, for *National Geographic* magazine. They sent each other bulletins about which cactus had put out a flower. Whereas Virginia walked through the garden and forgot the names, Trekkie was a keen botanist and enjoyed seeking out unusual specimens for the garden as much as Leonard. The Parsons were used to a slightly swankier lifestyle and one suspects that it was under Trekkie's influence that Leonard not only installed central heating, ordered new suits and more expensive wines but also started to order plants from specialist nurseries each year. Certainly a great number of plants from his garden notebooks under the heading 'ordered' date from the 1950s and 1960s. Perhaps it was also that he had more time for his garden.

Another shared passion was their pets. Leonard always had a dog and a couple of cats and his efforts to control them when they were on heat occasionally take on the character of a farce by Feydeau: 'There seems to be an animal on heat in every room. Zin shrieks all day in the apple room and I have to put her in the bathroom at night. Bess came on heat on Thursday but does not shriek, I'm glad to say. Coco will be the next, I suppose, and I should think it will be my turn after that, Delos is in great form; he got into the bathroom and pulled yards and yards of toilet paper off the rolls. I can see him at the moment in the garden; he has taken to spending a lot of time there, chasing birds, I think.'[1] Zin and Delos were Leonard's cats, Coco his dog; Bess was the Parsons' dog.

At last Leonard had someone to whom he could write about his garden: 'All the daffodils, crown imperials, & hyacinths in full bloom. The plum trees white. In the greenhouse the freesias a mass of flowers & the great red buds of the great lily bursting the sheath. But you've become so great a part of the garden & of me . . . that I feel it's wrong when the flowers come out when you're not here.'[2]

Leonard offered to extend the house further up into the attics after the war so that Trekkie could have the rest of the house and share one half of the garden with him 'which will, I hope, show you what I think of you . . . for there's no one else in the world to whom I'd give a square yard of it . . . & when I saw you digging potatoes or planting eucryphias on the other side of the imaginary fence, I would pass the time of day, as gardeners do . . .'[3] Trekkie refused. Playfully, Leonard suggested she share the house and just as charmingly she refused. Weekends at Rodmell were shared, leaving Leonard longing for more: 'Darling tiger, I *can't* help thinking of last week end & the difference you make to life, a house, the garden, me.'[4]

When the bombing of London grew more intense in August 1944, and Ian Parsons was posted to France, Trekkie moved into Monk's House for a year, with Ian's blessing. She and Leonard did not share a room. It is so hard to believe, reading their correspondence with twenty-first century sensibilities, that they did not sleep together, but it appears they did not. Indeed when problems with proving Leonard's will arose she had to swear so, under oath.

Trekkie started to make changes at Monk's House almost immediately, starting with 'the whole upheaval' of the kitchen. She painted Virginia's bedroom a pale pink and bought Vanessa's fabric to cover chairs. Pink was clearly a favourite colour: she wrote on 'passionate' pink paper and I wonder whether the large number of pink flowers which start to appear in the garden notebooks might have had something to do with her. In October 1944, the Parsons took a lease on Iford Grange, a large white house facing a most beautiful stretch of the Downs between Rodmell and Lewes. After the war they sold their London house and shared the first two floors of 24 Victoria Square with Leonard. It was a sophisticated arrangement, open between the parties concerned and exceptionally discreet as regards anyone else. Ian and Trekkie would go away on holiday together, with Ian flying home on the day Leonard would arrive to join Trekkie for a further week or so. Ian allowed Leonard to buy Trekkie a ring, and for her sixty-fourth birthday present the men shared the cost of a new coat, over £1,500 in today's money.

In 1946 Chatto & Windus absorbed the Hogarth Press, with Leonard retaining editorial control. Trekkie managed the domestic arrangements of two households with relative ease, charm and discretion, making both men happy yet apparently sleeping with neither of them. Perhaps the lack of sexual jealousy was the reason the arrangement worked without rancour. In 1977 Ian Parsons co-wrote and published *A Marriage of True Minds, An Intimate Portrait of Leonard and Virginia Woolf* in which not a word about Trekkie appears in the two-page epilogue covering the period in Leonard's life from 1941 to 1969.

Yet among close friends their relationship was not secret. When they were invited to Aldeburgh by Laurens van der Post, with whom Leonard often exchanged unusual plants, it was explained with regret that there was no room to accommodate 'old Ian' as well. There were other women hovering around Leonard, and he did not always rebuff the attention. Victoria Glendinning describes Leonard's garden as a 'honey-trap' where Leonard 'enchanted children, adolescents – and women'. Many contemporaries testify to his attractiveness to women. It was Trekkie though who remained the centre of his 'long and lovely autumn'.[5] They shared a life of gardening, pets, painting and writing at Monk's House, dovetailing and occasionally overlapping in a civilized fashion (they had many mutual friends) with Trekkie's life with Ian at Iford Grange, until Leonard died. Leonard continued with his political activities at home and abroad, writing his autobiography, reviewing books and making new friends. These included the actress Peggy Ashcroft, who was a frequent guest at Monk's House and the recipient, in 1962, of the gift of a pair of half standard apple trees. In 1967, Leonard was interviewed for BBC Television by Malcolm Muggeridge, both men seated in deckchairs on the lawn below the Millstone Terrace, a tree peony in flower behind them, to the accompaniment of birdsong and, faintly in the background, the strains of 'Eleanor Rigby' on a transistor radio. Speaking about Virginia, Leonard admitted that she was, for him, 'an integral part of the garden, she was so fond of it'.

A great deal of his time was of course taken up with handling Virginia's literary legacy, something he continued to work on daily until his death. He also managed to spend considerable amounts of time torturing various suppliers of goods and services. In 2001, when I gave my address to an elderly man behind the counter in the general hardware store in Lewes, he recalled a painful and protracted correspondence with Leonard concerning problems with his lawnmower. In 1951, Leonard was persuaded to open his garden for the National Garden Scheme for the first time, and continued to do so every year for the rest of his life; it was open the day before he suffered his stroke.

Leonard was fairly robust and fit until the year he died. His nephew Cecil remembers seeing him, aged 88, running down Victoria Street with a rucksack on his back to catch a bus. Then on the morning of 15 April 1969 Vout, the gardener, found Leonard in his upstairs sitting room, unable to speak properly. Louie was at home in her cottage, recovering from an operation for cancer (Leonard had visited her every day at Brighton Hospital), but she struggled over to Monk's House and refused to allow the ambulance men to take Leonard to hospital. 'I [knew] it would not be his wish.' A close circle gathered to look after Leonard in those last months – Trekkie, Louie and Annaliese West, who had married Louie's brother and was Trekkie's housekeeper in Kingston. Also

RIGHT Leonard's paper binder used to fascinate visitors and we enjoyed showing children how to make little books. Seedheads and autumnal foliage, together with medlars and quinces were displayed for visitors.

Virginia Browne-Wilkinson, a young author to whom he had become close and who helped him with his autobiography and letters, and Peggy Ashcroft. He was able to continue gardening and writing. Once he complained of dizzy spells, for which the doctor advised Leonard rest for two days, whereupon he would return to check up on him. On returning three days later the doctor found his patient on a ladder, pruning a fruit tree. 'You're late,' said Leonard.

Leonard died in the early hours of 14 August 1969, half a century to the day since he had stood on the lawn below bidding for Jacob Verrall's kale pots. Following his cremation everyone went back to 'his beautiful garden where time is suspended' and where Trekkie buried his ashes under the surviving elm on the edge of the Terrace – its partner having blown down in a gale shortly after Virginia's death.

When Leonard was approached to take part in the wonderfully absorbing BBC2 Omnibus documentary about Virginia Woolf, *A Night's Darkness, A Day's Sail*, he did not feel up to it but suggested instead that they interview Louie. Leonard always liked Louie, and left her a significant bequest in his will, enough to buy her own home. So it seems fitting to allow her to have the last word about Leonard: 'I stayed on at Monk's House to look after Mr Woolf during all the years that he was alone. He was always extremely busy: working at the Hogarth Press in London, going to political meetings, writing his books and, of course, looking after his garden. He loved his garden. With the help of Percy Bartholomew, his first gardener, he had made it a most beautiful place, full of flowers and fruit and vegetables. Mr Woolf was so active, he almost ran everywhere as though he needed more hours in the day, and he worked hard all the time. He really could work. He was also a very kind and thoughtful man . . .'[6]

ABOVE LEFT Leonard in his cactus house in the 1960s.
LEFT The creation of the bust of Leonard was an enjoyable affair. Commissioned by Virginia Browne-Wilkinson and Trekkie Parsons to stand on the wall along from the Tomlin bust of Virginia, it was sculpted over four weekends in the summer of 1968 by Charlotte Hewer, a young sculptress with an interest in gardens who went on to run a successful nursery in Chepstow. Charlotte remembers that he sat in the Orchard reading, 'which is why he is looking down', and that she knelt in the grass, which was 'full of daisies', to work. Trekkie had a tablet with these words carved into it placed under his bust on the flint wall facing the Orchard: 'I believe profoundly in two rules. Justice and mercy – they seem to me the foundation of all civilized life and society, if you include under mercy, toleration.'[7]
OPPOSITE Papyrus and cacti in the greenhouse today.

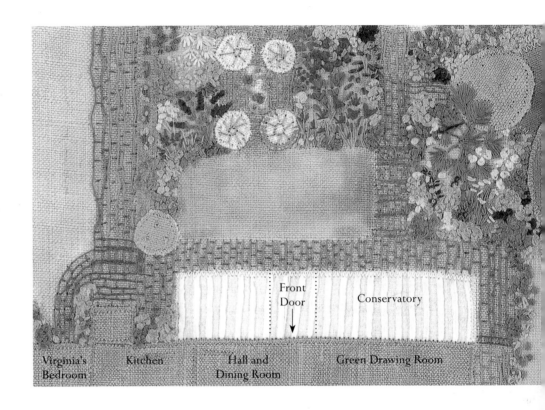

Virginia's Bedroom   Kitchen   Front Door   Conservatory   Hall and Dining Room   Green Drawing Room

The Rear Lawn Garden and Conservatory

In 1919 the rear façade of the house looked entirely different from the way it looks today. A small brick-built porch with a tile-hung roof surrounded the front door. Looking at the photograph opposite, the conservatory did not exist and the entire area was taken up with lawn. The path that runs through the centre of the conservatory now was a rolled ash path running in front of the house. The slope of the lawn was quite steep, a good spot for playing roly-poly, as Angelica Garnett and her cousin Judith Stephen would discover.

LEFT Leonard planted the Chusan palm the year before he died. Beyond it is the yew which was once the topiary on page 104. The steps were added by the National Trust, replacing treacherously slippery brick path, a necessary nod to the safety of visitors.

Vines and roses were established on the walls in 1919, but by the late 1930s the rear façade of the house was smothered in climbing plants. 'Monk's House is like a green cave, no light to eat by in the dining room, so we dine in the kitchen: this comes of the romantic profusion of our vine.'[1]

When Virginia writes about 'crossing the garden by the pale flowers'[2] to reach her bedroom at night I believe she is thinking about the 'clouds' of Japanese anemones at the foot of the creepers on the rear façade of the house.

The Conservatory was not added until the 1950s, thus was never seen by Virginia. Nigel Nicolson loathed the Conservatory. As he left the property he would dismiss it with a backwards wave, 'Hideous! Virginia would have hated it . . . should be pulled down.' I think had Virginia lived it would not have been built, but in Leonard's later years this 'miraculous immersion into the tropics'[3] afforded him and Trekkie enormous pleasure. A window in the green sitting room was converted into a narrow pair of doors leading into the southern end of the conservatory. Charlotte Hewer recalls white and yellow daturas, gloxinias, clivias and Scarborough lilies, natives of South Africa with bright orange trumpet flowers, very similar to hippeastrums, flowering in 1968. Today the bougainvillea and a grapevine tangle with plumbago on the walls, while clerodendrums,

OPPOSITE ABOVE The bed on the right of the Millstone Terrace, at the top of the steps. It is effectively one of two square island beds, so much harder to plan than a border with a backdrop.

OPPOSITE BELOW *Hydrangea arborescens* 'Annabelle' flourished in this shady spot.

RIGHT, CLOCKWISE FROM TOP LEFT *Monarda* 'Cambridge Scarlet'; I feel Leonard would have liked the tall and faintly sinister *Veronicastrum virginicum* 'Fascination' whose flower spikes emerge from a slowly unfurling tongue; *Buddleia davidii* 'Black Knight'; reliable agastache does earn its keep in a garden, with a long open season.

LEFT The rear façade of the house in the late 1930s. If you look closely you can just make out a statue in the niche: 'This morning Sandles brought Miranda, & she is now stood in her alcove.'

RIGHT The view of the Conservatory from the Italian Garden. The balcony above was added as an afterthought when Leonard carved his study out of the attic.

daturas and crinums share the space in the beds. Leonard's *Jasminum polyanthum* in flower scents the air from the gate. In the early part of the season every available space is covered with seedlings and dahlia cuttings.

Leonard continued to maintain the two large glasshouses in the Orchard – one for flowers and vegetables, a smaller greenhouse for tomatoes and one with a curving roof in which he kept his considerable collection of cacti for which he had developed a collector's passion by the 1940s, joining the National Cactus and Succulent Society. The main greenhouses were heated and for nearly twenty years it was Percy's unenviable job to stoke the boilers at 6.30am and 10.30pm every day. Copies of Leonard's orders to various suppliers testify to the number of specialist sands and grits required for growing cacti. A cactus in flower was a headline news item between Leonard and Trekkie: 'The cactuses – O I do wish you had seen them. One with eleven bright orange flowers all out & absolutely covering it in a brilliant crown & next to it another with four orange red flowers. And two of those cardinal's or bishop's mitre, one with a great flower on top white with delicate mauve lines & the other the palest of lemon yellow.'[4]

In 1919 there was one flower bed to the side of the lawn. When Leonard designed the Millstone Terrace in 1930 he included two new flower beds either side. It is the position of these flower beds, set above the sloping lawn, that makes the first sight of the garden at the back of the house so striking. The sun rises over the kitchen garden and works its way westwards, blazing through the flower beds until about two o'clock. Standing on the path by the Conservatory, or inside the front door, all the flowers in these beds seem backlit, almost incandescent.

OPPOSITE, CLOCKWISE FROM
TOP LEFT Leonard and Trekkie
would both have been familiar with
bougainvillea from their time in
Ceylon and South Africa; Crinum
lilies; cacti and succulents;
clerodendrums grew like weeds
at Monk's House, here reaching
up to the vine. One year a visitor
harvested all the grapes and
took them off to make some
wine, returning with a bottle the
following year.
RIGHT Tall, vanilla-scented crinum
lilies in the conservatory.

Part 6 After Leonard

In 1965 an American by the name of Mr Burlington Willes wrote to Leonard offering to buy Monk's House with the intention of managing it as a literary shrine. Leonard's response was crisp: 'I am afraid there is no question of Monk's House being made into a literary shrine as I shall leave it to someone else after my death.'[1] Unsurprisingly, that 'someone else' was Trekkie, to whom he left the bulk of his estate. Trekkie offered to donate all the papers of Leonard and Virginia if the University of Sussex would buy Monk's House at the probate value of £24,000. The University gave this proposal careful consideration. In particular there were concerns over whether the University would be able to provide adequate care for the house and garden. Nonetheless, the university took the papers, paid for the house and started to let it, with all of its contents, to visiting academic staff. Some appreciated this experience more than others. Professor Sharpringer and his wife Vivien, who took the black and white photographs of the interior in this book, loved the house and became friendly with Trekkie. Saul Bellow was too horrified by the primitive conditions to stay even a night to absorb any lingering inspiration in the ether.

ABOVE We bought this 1930s wheelbarrow and used it for the entire decade. The Trust bought it from us when we left.
OPPOSITE *Rosa* 'Félicité Perpétue' is the most versatile and obliging rose once it gets going.

Either way, these visiting academics were not required to look after the garden and the university ground staff tended only to the basic requirements. For nearly ten years the garden languished without proper care: fruit trees went unpruned, perennials died back, the kitchen garden was submerged by weeds, the ponds became thick with algae, pots and urns cracked and the topiary peacock lost its tail feathers. It is hard to understand why this was allowed to happen. A group of people started to express concern, in particular Vita's younger son, Nigel Nicolson, who was instrumental in bringing the National Trust and the university together in the late 1970s. Editing Virginia's letters at the time, he felt passionately that the house should be 'preserved as the Woolves knew it' and that 'The Trust have much more experience in running shrines.' I cannot help a shiver at the word, knowing how emphatic Leonard had been in responding to Mr Willes.

For two years, the Trust and Nigel Nicolson worked with people who had known the house during Leonard's and Virginia's lifetimes, including Trekkie, Quentin and Anne Olivier Bell, Angelica Garnett and Cecil and Marie Woolf. To begin with, the Trust's efforts were focused on 'interpreting' the house. It had been decided that it should be lived in and managed by tenants, so the upstairs rooms and those over the garages, as well as the lower half of the kitchen, would not be open to the public. Quentin and Angelica, Virginia's nephew and niece, painted lampshades and bases and the wooden screen drawn across the lower part of the kitchen when the house is open to visitors. Anne Olivier Bell donated Virginia's desk, which had been given to Quentin, for the writing lodge. Footage of Quentin at Charleston, recently unearthed, shows him sitting at this desk. Pictures were loaned or donated to the house, particularly by Trekkie, and the Trust bought the 1912 portrait of Virginia by Vanessa Bell. Fabrics were copied, paint colours recreated from scrapings found about the house and anything too fragile to be displayed, such as the tapestry mirror frame in the hallway, was painstakingly recreated. Textiles were repaired, paintings cleaned and restored. Many of the things on view today were in the house when Leonard died, were touched and used by him and by Virginia. What is missing, perhaps, is the mess and muddle of books, papers and pet food in dishes on the stairs, remembered by almost everyone who visited the Woolfs at Monk's House. Virginia's writing room today is set like a nun's cell, whereas we know that she worked in chaotic squalor, surrounded by papers and 'filth packets', her low-slung chair losing its stuffing. While I would not like to see an overly theatrical representation of the muddle, I always longed to add more books and papers to convey that this is a house where 'writing [was] done in flower-filled messy studios'.[2] It is a little too tidy perhaps, and the Woolfs' possessions more artfully arranged, and yet none of this matters because the ways in which visitors engage with the house physically, treading the same brick steps, banging their heads on the low doorways, sniffing the damp in the sitting room

LEFT The steps leading from the kitchen to the garden.

and gazing out at the view across the garden – these have not changed in almost a century and so create the strongest connection to Leonard and Virginia.

In the garden the restoration team faced a far greater challenge. I would give much to have been with them in 1980 to make a formal note of what survived. However neglected and overgrown the garden may have been it was still the closest to what Leonard left behind. But I suspect there was a feeling that with Leonard's death and the passing of so many years, the garden too had faded away and that the best that could be done was to tidy it into an acceptable state for opening and perhaps look at the interpretation as time went by. Perhaps the Trust also felt that people would come to see Virginia's house and not Leonard's garden.

It was decided that, henceforth, the incoming tenant would be responsible for the upkeep of the garden, with advice from the Trust's garden adviser. This seems to have been the reason behind labour-saving measures such as turfing over the long border on the Terrace and the borders just inside the Orchard. By the time the university acquired the house, the glasshouse with the curved roof, containing Leonard's collection of cacti, had been taken down and the small tomato house had been given to Annaliese West. It is thought that Trekkie may have given away the collection of cacti and possibly the recipient removed the glasshouse as well. Adrian Orchard and Ian Jeffrey, Rodmell villagers at the time, were responsible for rescuing and restoring the vegetable garden. They made use of the large greenhouse until it was deemed unsafe, when the university had it dismantled.

The Trust decided not to pursue a faithful historic recreation of the planting. Presumably, Trekkie was asked for her advice although a note of a meeting with her in 1995 is not particularly revealing, other than to mention the *Hydrangea petiolaris* on the front wall of the house. For two years the Trust gardeners worked to prepare the garden for opening in 1982. Different tenants came and went, the first few not staying long enough to make a mark on the garden. In 1984 a young couple, Allan and Martina Parkes, both opera singers working at Glyndebourne, became the first tenants to stay for any length of time. They celebrated their wedding in the garden, and their two sons were born in the house. They started to research the garden using Leonard's papers at the university and worked incredibly hard, with help from the Trust, to get the garden looking very good again by the time they left in 1993.

Thereafter the status quo was more or less kept for a few years, until a period of about three years when there was no long-term tenant and the garden slipped back a little. On our arrival, we found that certain thuggish perennials, notably white phlox, had elbowed their way through the borders. With Virginia's 'we are watering the earth with our money' ringing in our ears, we increased the variety of shrubs and herbaceous plants, replaced old lavenders and fruit trees and planted numerous roses. Allowing a tenant to tend and maintain a garden open to the public is, for the National Trust, a practical compromise and a gamble. Mainly, it wants the tenant to keep the garden neat and presentable. With regard to planting however the Trust recognises that it cannot be too prescriptive; after

all, the tenant pays for the cost of the plants and maintenance. We received advice from the National Trust garden adviser, who visited once a year for the first four years and then left us alone. There was no obligation placed upon us to research the garden. In our lease there were guidelines: we could not change the layout of the garden, or remove trees. With regard to the borders we were advised to garden 'in the spirit of Bloomsbury'.

There are people who remember the garden when Leonard was alive; some are adamant that it has changed beyond all recognition and others feel that considering the history and the lapse of time, it retains much of the same feel. In 2001 a german student called Eva Wacker wrote a dissertation on the garden, with suggestions as to how it could be restored to reflect only the period 1926–41. I dread this approach. It seems to me the same thing as death for a garden to be pinned to a moment in time. Leonard lived on at Monk's House for twenty-eight years after Virginia died, each year increasing his level of horticultural skill and expertise. The influence of Trekkie cannot and should not be discounted. One of the aspects of the garden most enjoyed by visitors is that it is 'full of atmosphere' and 'alive – not frozen in time'. Perhaps a better approach would be to restore some of the vertical accents such as the three Lombardy poplars ranged in a line across the Terrace (there are only two), the cherry trees in the Walled Garden, the *Eucryphia* x *nymansensis* in the lawn and the yews along the edge of the terrace. I would like to see the yew in the Italian garden gradually reduced and the topiary reinstated. Leonard kept the orchard neat and close cropped and the flint walls bare of creepers.

As for the herbaceous planting, we have ample evidence that Leonard liked new and exciting plants. He rarely bought the same thing twice. He did not plant borders with colour themes or plant in threes, fives and sevens. He bought single plants and filled up the borders with annuals, particularly zinnias. He grew vast white lilies, nerines and crinums. He liked his lawns tidy and edged up but wasn't quite so fussy about weeds. He did like bright colours but he also loved white flowers. He packed his spring garden with wallflowers, forget-me-nots and unusual bulbs. He loved roses but detested floribundas. I think of Leonard's gardening as cottage garden in approach but with more sophisticated plants, exotic even. He loved his orchard and vegetables, and his greenhouses full of cacti and tropical plants. These known likes and dislikes, coupled with endless lists of plant names and glimpses in Virginia's diaries and letters, are all we have to go on. The rest is up to whoever is planting and maintaining the garden at any particular time. For ten, happy years, that was us.

THIS PAGE Our lease required us to place arrangements of fresh flowers in each room open to visitors. This was an obligation I enjoyed sharing with Maggy Tyhurst, who worked as the conservation assistant at Monk's House for more than twenty years until we left. Maggy brought something indefinable to the house and her flower arrangements were often complimented by visitors on comment cards.

Thoughts from behind the screen

When the house is open to the public, a screen is pulled across the lower half of the kitchen. We would work in the garden until the house opened at 2pm and repair to lunch behind the screen from where we could hear the visitors talking as they walked through the house.

One of the most upsetting assumptions reiterated by them, as they made their way into the garden through the kitchen door to get to Virginia's bedroom, was that the marriage between Leonard and Virginia 'must have been cold because she couldn't even bear to sleep in the same house' or, worse, 'I suppose she needed to be separate for all her lesbian affairs'. I would sit behind the screen, gritting my teeth, longing to pop my head out and put them right. Now is my opportunity to do so.

In Virginia's letters and diaries, I perceive an extremely successful marriage, with a level of closeness and intimacy which couples who start married life with more successful bedroom encounters might struggle to achieve. In twenty-nine years of marriage Leonard and Virginia were barely apart. When they were, their letters were playful, flirtatious and intensely affectionate with the use of animal nicknames and anticipation of 'nuzzling' and 'nibbling' on reuniting. They found each other beautiful. Virginia had once posed the question 'What do you think is probably the happiest moment in one's whole life?' and then answered it herself, thus 'I think it's the moment when one is walking in one's garden, perhaps picking off a few dead flowers, and suddenly one thinks: My husband lives in that house – And he loves me.'[1] Returning from a visit to Vita at Long Barn, she wrote 'A very nice homecoming . . . It has not been dull – my marriage; not at all'.[2] Victoria Glendinning suggests that Leonard might not have appreciated the full extent of the relationship between Vita and Virginia until he read Virginia's diaries after her death. I think it is also possible that he of all people knew that Virginia was unlikely to have a successful sexual relationship with anyone (although Vita was her best shot), and thus the marriage was never under threat. As Virginia herself put it, writing in her diary about her affair with Vita 'so we go on - a spirited, creditable affair, I think, innocent (spiritually) &, all gain, I think; rather a bore for Leonard, but not enough to worry him. The truth is one has room for a good many relationships.'[3] Yet it is clear that Leonard was the centre of her existence. She had complete trust in his judgment, even when she occasionally expressed disappointment, fury even, in having to eschew parties or too much excitement. When he was ill, she enjoyed looking after him for a change. For all her feminist beliefs, she liked being married and enjoyed home-making. Her diary entries about their childlessness, self-imposed because of her illness, are heart-breaking. In October 1937, Virginia was considering a visit to Vanessa in Paris, worrying about her still after the recent death of Julian. Leonard demurred. In her diary she wrote 'Then I was overcome with happiness . . we walked round the square love making – after 25 years can't bear to be separate . . . you see it is an enormous pleasure, being wanted: a wife. And our marriage so complete.'[4]

A mutual respect for fine mental furniture had a great deal to do with their happiness; that, and their work together in the Hogarth Press, their political

sympathies and, perhaps most of all, the devoted way in which Leonard looked after Virginia when she was ill. As she wrote in her last letter to Leonard, 'I don't think two people could have been happier than we have been'.[5] Having lived in the home they loved so much, it is important to me that people appreciate this.

When we arrived at Monk's House we knew very little about Virginia. To begin with, I found the intensity of some of the visitors disconcerting. On a day when the house was closed, I came home to find a woman weeping at the gate, overcome by the thought that Virginia's hand had touched that very gate as she left the house on her way to the river. I did not have the heart to tell her that Virginia had left the garden through a different gate at the top of the garden, long since disused. Instead I made soothing noises and offered to make her a cup of tea. On another day when we were closed, I looked up from my work and noticed two women walking up the flower walk, arm in arm. I opened the window, about to call out that we were closed, when I realised they were now embracing, weeping, overwhelmed by finding themselves in Virginia's garden. I could always spot the visitors on a pilgrimage. They lingered longer in the rooms, looked at the house through their own eyes rather than the screens of their mobile phones, and were often to be found sitting quietly on a bench at closing time, absorbing the atmosphere. We enjoyed sharing Monk's House with these people, understanding that it had become, after all, a literary shrine and we were its temporary keepers. Having fallen under Virginia's spell myself, I came to prefer the weeping women to the visitors who left us quite without an answer to the question 'so why were people so afraid of her then?', or 'are those her cats?'

It has been two years since we left Monk's House and yet, writing this book, I have found myself able to reach out in my mind to every corner of the garden, embroidering my way through the flowerbeds as though we had left only yesterday. Re-reading Virginia's diaries and letters I realise how little has changed in almost a century. When she announces that she is going to stop writing and go to pick a 'leaf full of strawberries'[6] for supper, I move through the garden with her. I know that the door of her writing lodge sticks slightly when she closes it behind her. She steps down on to the brick terrace and then on to the grass, always slightly crunchier under the chestnut tree outside her lodge. In the vegetable garden the air is soft and pungent. She stops to take in her view across the water meadows, with only birdsong and lowing cattle breaking the silence. She walks back to the house. The bumps in the orchard grass, the uneven brick path, the foliage of the borders brushing her clothes, the stoop she makes as she bends down to go through the kitchen door, the adjustment to the different light in the house – none of these things has changed. Virginia and Leonard have themselves been absorbed into the 'tranquil atmosphere' of the house and garden. This atmosphere is not diminished because the planting in the borders is different and some trees have blown down or grown taller. The soul of the garden, which drew the Woolfs to it in 1919, is, I believe, still there.

RIGHT Our cats, Handlebars and Boy, who came to the house as kittens, kept the mice and rabbits at bay and were frequent recipients of praise on the visitor comment cards.

Sources for Quotations

Abbreviations used:

Love Letters – *Love Letters: Leonard Woolf and Trekkie Ritchie Parsons 1941–1968* ed. Judith Adamson, Chatto & Windus 2001

LVW-I – Nigel Nicolson assisted by Joanne Trautmann (ed) *The Flight of the Mind The Letters of Virginia Woolf Volume I 1888–1912*

LVW-II – Nigel Nicolson assisted by Joanne Trautmann (ed) *The Question of Things Happening The Letters of Virginia Woolf Volume II 1912–1922*

LVW-III – Nigel Nicolson assisted by Joanne Trautmann (ed) *A Change of Perspective The Letters of Virginia Woolf Volume III 1923–1928*

LVW-IV – Nigel Nicolson assisted by Joanne Trautmann (ed) *A Reflection of the Other Person The Letters of Virginia Woolf Volume IV 1929–1931*

LVW-V – Nigel Nicolson assisted by Joanne Trautmann (ed) *The Sickle Side of the Moon The Letters of Virginia Woolf Volume I 1932–1935*

LVW-VI – Nigel Nicolson assisted by Joanne Trautmann (ed) *Leave the Letters till We're Dead The Letters of Virginia Woolf Volume I 1936–1941*

LW-AB1 – *Sowing An Autobiography of the Years 1880-1904* Leonard Woolf

LW-AB2 – *Growing An Autobiography of the Years 1904–1911* Leonard Woolf

LW-AB3 – *Beginning Again An Autobiography of the Years 1911–1918* Leonard Woolf

LW-AB4 – *Downhill all the Way An Autobiography of the Years 1919–1939* Leonard Woolf

LW-AB5 – *The Journey not the Arrival Matters An Autobiography of the Years 1939–1969* Leonard Woolf

LW-Letters – *Letters of Leonard Woolf* ed Frederic Spotts Harcourt Brace Jovanovich 1989

Recollections – *Recollections of Virginia Woolf* edited and with an introduction by Joan Russell Noble

VWD-I – Anne Olivier Bell assisted by Andrew MacNeillie (ed), *The Diary of Virginia Woolf Volume I 1915–1919*

VWD-II – Anne Olivier Bell assisted by Andrew MacNeillie (ed), *The Diary of Virginia Woolf Volume II 1920–1924*

VWD-III – Anne Olivier Bell assisted by Andrew MacNeillie (ed), *The Diary of Virginia Woolf Volume III 1925–1930*

VWD-IV – Anne Olivier Bell assisted by Andrew MacNeillie (ed), *The Diary of Virginia Woolf Volume IV 1931–1935*

VWD-V – Anne Olivier Bell assisted by Andrew MacNeillie (ed), *The Diary of Virginia Woolf Volume V 1936–1941*

Introduction (pages 8–11)
p8 display quote LW-AB4 p14
1 LW-AB4 p15

Finding Monk's House (pages 16–21)
1 University of Sussex, Monk's House Archive
2 LVW-I no. 546
3 VWD-I 3 July 1919
4 LW-AB3 page 62
5 VWD-I 3 July 1919
6 LVW-II no 1069

Settling In (pages 22–33)
1 LVW-II no 1081
2 VWD-II 2 August 1920
3 LVW-II no 1110
4 LVW-II no 1146
5 LVW-II no 689
6 LW-Letters 8 September 1918 to Margaret Llewelyn Davies p 221
7 LVW-II no 1082
8 VWD-II 31 May 1920
9 VWD-II 8 August 1921
10 LVW-II no 1187
11 LVW-II no 1249
12 LVW-II no 1182
13 VWD-III 22 September 1925
14 LVW-III no 1164
15 LVW-III no 1644
16 University of Sussex, Monk's House papers, unpublished 10 August 1926
17 VWD-III 22 September 1928
p32 display quote VWD-III 9 June 1926
18 VWD-II 15 September 1926

The Orchard (pages 34–43)
1 LVW-II no 1139
2 LVW-III no 1911
p35 display quote LW-Letters page 288
p36 display quote LVW-II no 1240

3 LW-Letters page 288
4 LVW-VI no 3654
5 LVW-III no 1706
6 LW-Letters p243
7 LVW-III no 1970
8 LVW-III no 1794
9 *The Waves*
10 LVW-V no 2634
11 LW-AB5 p187
12 VWD-II 2 January 1923
13 VWD-IV 13 June 1932
14 VWD-II 1 October 1920

The Fig Tree Garden (pages 44–51)
1 LVW-III no 1918
2 LVW-II no 1182
3 VWD-II 15 September 1921
4 VWD-III 8 December 1929
5 LVW-II no 1288

New Rooms in the Garden (pages 52–57)
1 LW-AB4 p145
2 LVW-III no 515
3 *Memoirs of Lady Ottoline Morrell*
4 Katherine Mansfield, quoted in *Hortus Revisited: A Twenty-first birthday anthology* ed David Wheeler p146

The Millstone Terrace (pages 58–63)
p61 display quote VWD-III 5 September 1926
1 University of Sussex, Monk's House Papers
2 LVW-III no 1921
p62 display quote LVW-VI no 3155
3 VWD-I 3 July 1919

The Fish Pond Garden (pages 64–71)
1 LVW-VI no 3324
2 VWD-IV 23 September 1933

3 The Provost and Scholars of King's College, Cambridge and The Society of Authors as the E.M. Forster Estate.

4 VWD-III 5 August 1929

5 LVW-IV no 2063

6 VWD-IV 7 August 1931

7 Love Letters no 52

Virginia's Bedroom Garden (pages 72–87)

1 LVW-IV nos 1993 and 1996

2 VWD-III 28 March 1929

3 LVW-VI no 3349

p74 display quote VWD-III 25 November 1929

4 LVW-IV nos 2016 2020

5 LVW-VI no 3099

6 VWD-III 8 September 1930

7 LVW-IV no 2236

8 LVW-IV no 2237

9 Recollections p159

10 LVW-IV no 2194

11 *Moments of Being* p 67

12 VWD-III 21 February 1930

13 VWD-III 2 October 1929

14 VWD-IV 19 September 1931

The Flower Walk (pages 88–99)

1 VWD-II 14 September 1921

2 VWD-II 7 September 1922

3 VWD-III 22 September 1929

4 LVW-I no 380

5 LVW-III no 1575

6 LVW-II no 1087

7 LVW-III no 1760

8 LVW-VI no 3293

The Italian Garden (pages 100–107)

1 LVW-V no 2703

2 LVW-V no 2736

3 VWD-IV 2 September 1933

4 VWD-IV 10 September 1933

5 LVW-V no 2799

6 Nigel Nicolson, *Virginia Woolf* p62

7 VWD-IV 26 September 1933

8 LVW-VI no 3264

The Terrace (pages 108–115)

1 VWD-III 26 September 1926

2 VWD-III 25 September 1929

3 VWD-III 5 September 1926

4 VWD-V 9 August 1939

5 LVW-V no 2770

6 VWD-IV 30 September 1931

7 Letter of Lytton Strachey, 21 August 1909

8 VWD-III 14 December 1929

9 LW-AB4 p 183

10 LVW-VI no 3128

11 VWD-V 17 August 1937

The Writing Lodge (pages 116–125)

1 VWD-IV 5 October 1934

2 VWD-IV 26 November 1934

3 LVW-III no 1921

4 LW-AB4 p52

5 LW-AB4 p52

6 LVW-IV no 2244

7 LVW-VI no 3155

8 LVW-VI no 3173

9 LVW-VI no 3141

10 LVW-VI no 3153

11 *Moments of Being* p 66

12 VWD-V 2 March 1937

13 VWD-V 9 April 1937

14 Letter from Vanessa Bell to Vita Sackville-West, 2 April 1941

15 LVW-VI no 3294

16 LW-AB4 p9

17 VWD-IV 13 June 1932

p124 display quote VWD-IV 13 June 1932

The Walled Garden (pages 126–139)

1 LW-AB3 p64

2 LVW-VI no 3303

3 University of Sussex, Monk's House papers

4 LVW-VI no 3324

5 VWD-V 25 October 1937

p132 display quote LVW-VI no 3293

6 VWD-V 19 July 1937

7 LVW-VI no 3440

8 LVW-VI no 3454

The Last Page (pages 140–153)

1 LVW-VI no 3429

2 LVW-VI no 3429

3 VWD-V 10 September 1938

4 LVW-VI no 3545

p142 display quote LW-Letters Spotts p250

5 VWD-V 28 July 1939

6 LVW-VI no 3536

7 LVW-VI no 3582

8 VWD-V 24 March 1940

9 VWD-V 13 & 15 May 1940

p147 display quote VWD-V 19 February 1940

10 LVW-VI no 3650

11 LVW-VI no 3643

12 VWD-V 16 December 1940

13 VWD-V 2 October 1940

14 VWD-V 16 December 1940

15 LVW-VI no 3689

16 VWD-V 29 December 1940

17 VWD-V 15 January 1941

18 VWD-V 15 January 1941

19 LW-Letters Spotts p250

20 VWD-V 24 March 1941

21 University of Sussex, Leonard Woolf Papers

The Vegetable Garden (pages 154–157)

1 Recollections p85

After Virginia (pages 158–167)

1 Love Letters no 333

2 Love Letters no 152

3 Love Letters no 98

4 Love Letters no 134

5 Letter from Quentin Bell to Trekkie Parsons 28 August 1969, quoted in *Leonard Woolf, A Life* by Victoria Glendinning p491

6 Recollections p162

7 LW-AB5 p167

The Rear Lawn Garden and Conservatory (pages 168–175)

1 LVW-VI 3286

2 VWD-IV 7 August 1931

3 Julian Bell in *Virginia Woolf's Rodmell: An illustrated guide to a Sussex Village* ed Maire McQueeney 1991

4 Love Letters no 171

After Leonard (pages 176–183)

1 LW-Letters p539

2 John Lehmann in Recollections p 41

Thoughts from Behind the Screen (pages 184–187)

1 George Spater and Ian Parsons *A Marriage of True Minds* Harcourt Brace Jovanovich 1977 p 62

2 VWD-III 26 July 1930

3 VWD-III 23 November 1926

4 VWD-V 22 October 1937

5 Virginia's last letter to Leonard, left for him on the sitting room mantelpiece on Friday, 28 March 1941

6 LVW-VI no 3264

Acknowledgements (page 192)

caption LVW-III no 1760

Bibliography

All quotations are cited within the text. Below is a list of the books about Virginia and Leonard Woolf which have been constant companions over the past ten years.

Victoria Glendinning *Leonard Woolf, A Life* Simon & Schuster 2004

Hermione Lee *Virginia Woolf* Chatto & Windus 1996

Nigel Nicolson assisted by Joanne Trautmann (ed) *The Letters of Virginia Woolf Vols 1-6* Chatto & Windus (1975-1980)

George Spater and Ian Parsons *A Marriage of True Minds* Harcourt Brace Jovanovich 1977

Letters of Leonard Woolf edited by Frederic Spotts Harcourt Brace Jovanovich 1989

Anne Olivier Bell assisted by Andrew MacNeillie (ed), *The Diary of Virginia Woolf (vols 1-5)* Chatto & Windus (1975-1980)

Recollections of Virginia Woolf edited and with an introduction by Joan Russell Noble

John Lehmann *Thrown to the Woolfs* Weidenfeld & Nicolson 1978

Katherine C. Hill-Miller *From the Lighthouse to Monk's House: A guide to Virginia Woolf's Literary Landscapes* Gerald Duckworth & Co 2001

Vanessa Curtis (foreword by Professor Julia Briggs) *Virginia Woolf's Women* Sutton Publishing Limited 2003

Ruth Webb *Virginia Woolf* The British Library 2000

Julie Singleton *A History of Monk's House and the Village of Rodmell*

Nigel Nicolson *Virginia Woolf* Weidenfeld & Nicolson 2000

Alison Light *Mrs Woolf and the Servants* Fig Tree (Penguin Group) 2007

Moments of Being Virginia Woolf Unpublished Autobiographical Writings edited and with an introduction and notes by Jeanne Schulkind

Leonard Woolf, an autobiography in five volumes:
Sowing 1880–1904
Growing 1904–1911
Beginning Again 1911–1918
Downhill all the Way 1919–1939
The Journey not the Arrival Matters 1939–1969

Ruth Webb *Virginia Woolf* British Library Lives 2000

Monk's House Garden: The country home of Leonard and Virginia Woolf in Sussex History, Development and Restoration (2000) - A dissertation by Eva Wacker

The Virginia Woolf Society of Great Britain
www.virginiawoolfsociety.co.uk

Monk's House is open to the public. For opening hours and all other information please refer to www.nationaltrust.org.uk.

For anyone with an interest in the life, works and times of the Bloomsbury Group, the Bloomsbury Heritage monographs are invaluable. In particular:

Julie Singleton *A History of Monk's House and Village of Rodmell*

Dr Nuala Hancock *Gardens in the Work of Virginia Woolf*

Diana Gardner *The Rodmell Papers, Reminiscences of Virginia and Leonard Woolf by a Sussex Neighbour*

Key to 1919 garden plan (opposite, above)

1 The Street

2 Site of the old cess pool

3 Before the extension was built in 1929, this area of garden was full of fruit trees and vegetable beds. A window was set in the north-facing wall, bricked in when the extension was built.

4 This parcel of land was not part of the 1919 conveyance; Leonard acquired it in 1920 and it later became the Italian garden. A small parsonage stood here until it was demolished in 1856. I believe the yew tree may well have been in the garden of the parsonage. It is an odd place to have planted one otherwise.

5 Yew tree

6 Church Lane

7 The earth closet, in its glade of cherry laurels

8 The laundry was large enough to have its own chimney stack, which blew off the roof in 1922.

9 Note there was no conservatory. The rolled ash path followed the house and then 'strikes off' up towards the garden.

10 The remains of an old granary. I believe the granary ran up to the orchard with access to the orchard by way of a wooden gate.

11 The 'ancient fig tree'.

12 The old tool shed, which Virginia and Leonard converted into a writing room.

13 There has always been an outbuilding here, now the garden shed.

14 Small outbuilding

15 The lych gate of St Peter's, Rodmell stands here, and Jacob Verrall is buried just beyond it, the first grave on the right.

16 The graveyard of St Peter's, Rodmell

17 Laurel hedge planted by Caroline Verrall in 1882, and removed by Leonard in 1920.

18 Lower portion of Pound Croft field. Note that the upper portion stands about 4.5m (15 feet) above, with a steep bank between.

19 The two elms, 'Leonard' and 'Virginia'

20 Pound Croft field ('the Croft'). This served as the village green and was used for games of stool ball and cricket.

Key to 1932 garden plan (opposite, below)

1 Extension added in 1929

2 Note the Italian Garden is still lawn in 1932

3 The Millstone Terrace

4 This area was used for growing vegetables as well.

5 Mowings pit

6 Vegetable Garden

7 Fruit cage

8 Gate at the top of the garden. It is almost certain that this was the gate through which Virginia went on her last walk to the Ouse.

9 Five yew trees were ranged along the edge of the terrace. These must have been planted later than 1930. Two of them are visible in the photograph of the bowling match on page 143.

10 Hawthorn hedges planted to shelter the vegetable garden. Only the short limb remains.

11 The Bowling Lawn

12 The Dewpond

13 The Terrace

14 No flower beds are indicated here, but soon after 1930 Leonard created the long border along the north side of the flint walls which can be seen in the photograph on page 110.

15 Gate from the lower end of the Croft. Cart loads of manure were delivered through this gate.

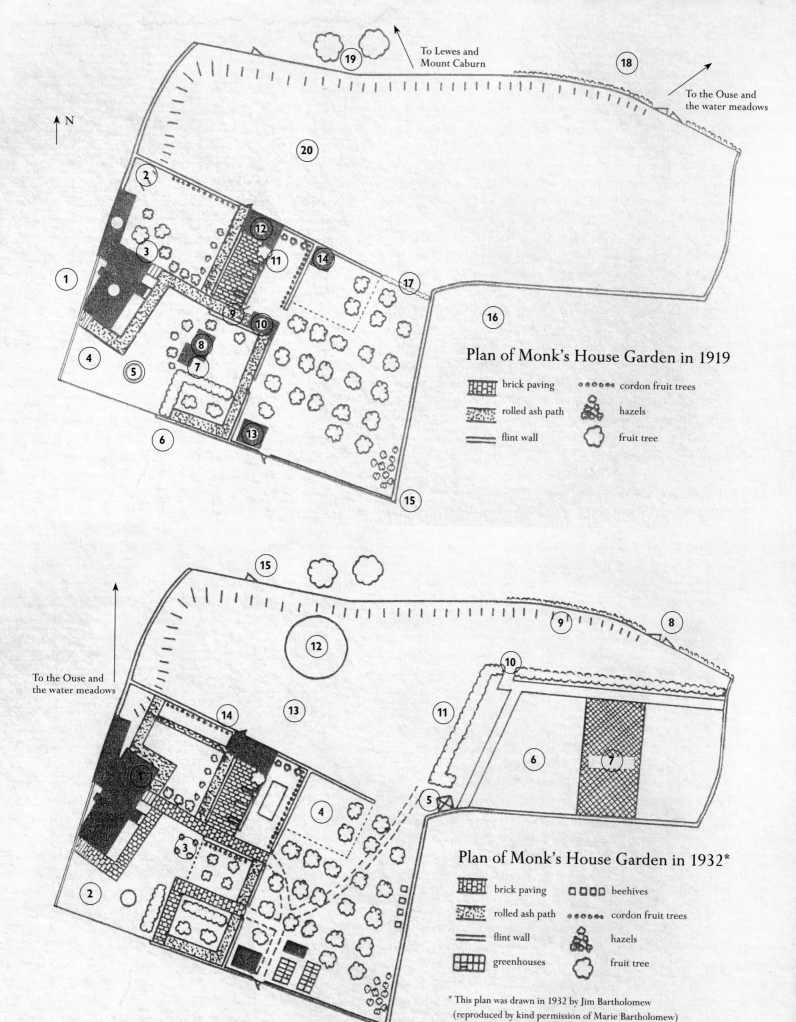

To Lewes and
Mount Caburn

To the Ouse and
the water meadows

N

Plan of Monk's House Garden in 1919

	brick paving		cordon fruit trees
	rolled ash path		hazels
	flint wall		fruit tree

To the Ouse and
the water meadows

Plan of Monk's House Garden in 1932*

	brick paving		beehives
	rolled ash path		cordon fruit trees
	flint wall		hazels
	greenhouses		fruit tree

* This plan was drawn in 1932 by Jim Bartholomew
(reproduced by kind permission of Marie Bartholomew)

LEFT 'My dear Julian, Could you possibly show your good heart by bringing me back fifty Voltigeur cigars? in a box. One declares them, and they make no fuss.' Virginia got the habit of smoking cigars in Italy and could never break it.

Author's acknowledgements

Leaving a tiny garden in London to find ourselves responsible for the garden at Monk's House was exciting, but also daunting. Our lease required us to employ a gardener for one day a week. We found Mel Osborne as we moved in, and for ten years we worked together on the garden, joined later by Janet Magill, a volunteer, and Chris Sawyer, who helped Jonathan with the endless mowing. We all learned the garden together, made maps for the spring bulbs, divided and propagated perennials, sowed annuals, lifted dahlias, transplanted seedlings, tidied sheds and weeded paths. It was a shared enterprise and they were all a pleasure to work with.

I would like to thank the following people for their help in the research and preparation for this book:

The staff at the University of Sussex Special Collections who assisted me with the Monk's House Papers and Leonard Woolf Archive. Jeremy Crow and Sarah Burton from the Society of Authors, and Sarah McMahon from The Random House Group. It means a great deal to me that Cecil Woolf has written the foreword for this book. I am grateful to Dr Ruth Webb and Professor Simon Keynes for helping to track down the image of Leonard and Virginia on page 37. Thanks also to Allison Pritchard and Chris Rowlin of The National Trust. I am grateful to Julie Singleton for sharing her research into the history of Monk's House so generously and to Miranda Money and Vanessa Curtis for reading the manuscript and offering valuable advice. Thanks also to Charlotte (Hewer) Evans, Adrian Orchard, Ian Jeffrey and Marie Bartholomew for sharing their memories of the Woolfs and the garden. I would like to thank Adam Nicolson for allowing me to spend a magical afternoon at Sissinghurst sifting through photograph albums in search of images of Monk's House garden. Thanks also to Dr Wendy Hitchmough of the Charleston Trust for her help and advice on various matters.

Thanks to: Dottie Owens and Jim Marshall, formerly of the National Trust, for sharing their considerable knowledge about Monk's House; Lorna Brown for her beautiful watercolour illustrations; and Jacqui Small, Joanna Copestick, Lydia Halliday and Alexandra Labbe Thompson at Jacqui Small Publishing LLP. In particular, Caroline Arber and I are grateful to Sian Parkhouse and Maggie Town for their skill, creativity and patience.

I gratefully acknowledge the following individuals, institutions and organisations for the sight of or use of material, or permission to quote from material in copyright: the University of Sussex, and the Society of Authors as their representative, for published and unpublished material by Leonard Woolf, and for extracts from Leonard Woolf's *Sowing, Growing, Beginning Again, Downhill all the Way* and *The Journey Not the Arrival Matters*; © Estate of Vanessa Bell, courtesy Henrietta Garnett for the paintings by Vanessa Bell and Angelica Garnett on pages 97, 115 and 142; David Higham Associates (for John Lehmann); the Provost and Scholars of King's College, Cambridge, and the Society of Authors as the literary representatives of the E.M. Forster estate; The Random House Group Ltd for *The Letters of Virginia Woolf* ed. Nigel Nicolson and Joanne Trautmann, Hogarth Press, for *The Diary of Virginia Woolf* ed. Anne Olivier Bell, Hogarth Press, *Moments of Being* by Virginia Woolf, Hogarth Press, *Love Letters: Leonard Woolf and Trekkie Ritchie Parsons* 1941-1968 ed. Judith Adamson, Chatto & Windus; Julian Bell (for the estate of Professor Quentin Bell) for the extract on page 164; © the representatives of the estate of Trekkie Ritchie Parsons for the painting on page 25.

Every effort has been made to contact all persons having any rights regarding the material used in this book.

Photographer's acknowledgements

With thanks to Gabi Tubbs for her art direction in the photographs on the following pages: 20, 22, 23, 24 ,31, 32-33, 75, 122-123, 130-131, 133.

Archive image acknowledgements

Pages 7, 51, 110 (top): By kind permission of Adam Nicolson
Page 16: © Tate, London 2013

The following images are reproduced from the Monk's House Albums by kind permission of the Harvard Theatre Collection, the Houghton Library and the Society of Authors as the representatives of the Woolf Estates. The MS and image numbers are given in brackets for each image where available:
Page 18 (unmarked folder)
Page 47 (1754/8159 and 8161)
Page 61 (box 2/7)
Page 67 *left* (1794/8145), *right* (MH3(89))
Page 68 (MH-3, 33)
Page 79 (1794/8302)
Page 104 (1795/1116)
Page 115 (1795/1183)
Page 119 (box 2, unmarked folder)
Page 143 *right* (1795/1435)
Page 146 (box 2, unmarked folder)
Page 161 *bottom* (1795/0923)
Page 172 (1795/1115)

Pages 25, 26,30 (*bottom*): © Vivienne Sharpringer, 1970
Page 37: By kind permssion of the Keynes family
Page 110 (*bottom*): © The British Library Board / ADD.50522f318
Pages 114, 130, 143 (*left*): John Lehmann, author of *Thrown to the Woolfs*, published by Weidenfeld & Nicolson
Pages 158, 166: University of Sussex and The Society of Authors as their representative